MOUNT ATHOS
The highest place on earth

METROPOLITAN NIKOLAOS
of Mesogaia

MOUNT ATHOS
The highest place on earth

Translated by
Caroline Makropoulos

EN PLO
editions

© EN PLO Editions
49 Kolokotroni str.
Athens 105 60
Tel: +30 210 3226343
Fax : +30 210 3221238
e-mail: info@enploeditions.gr
www.enploeditions.gr

First edition: December 2007

ISBN: 978 - 960 6719- 17 - 2

CONTENTS

Thoughts of the Translator

This is no ordinary travel book, although at first it may appear so. The author is bound on an inner journey of the soul and the heart as much as an outward journey. His is a journey of discovery into the soul: it is a discovery of self and of his vocation, something at first he so little suspects and so vehemently tries to reject.

Just as the author is startled by the ascetics who emerge suddenly out of their hiding places in the Athonite desert, so too are we startled by the newness and originality of his thought and manner of expression, his language and his way of looking at things. He and the characters he meets use images and metaphors from science, and especially from physics, to talk about the world of the spirit, challenging us to review and reappraise our conception of 'saints' and 'saintliness' and surprising us with visions of the heavenly in the here and now of this physical world.

There is also the natural world of Athos, which so often reflects and harmonizes with the inner realm of the spirit, and concomitantly sometimes even enters into the heart, becoming one with and transfiguring it.

Hard as it may be to take in, this is a world of the unexpected, where things are not always as they seem: when we look at a rubbish tip we may actually not only be looking up at the stars, but we may be looking at the stars themselves; and when we meet a fool, or a 'wild ascetic', we may actually be meeting a man of great holiness, a saint.

This is seemingly a world of the strange and of the unusual that we may find unreal and unbelievable, offensive even: skulls and skeletons, angels and the fragrance of 'holy relics'. Yet this is the tradition that is Athos, this is the holy tradition that is Christian Orthodoxy: these are *living* and *lived* realities. For in Christian Orthodoxy death is part of life just as much as life is part of death. At the Easter service of the Resurrection we sing 'Christ is Risen from the dead, trampling down death by death, and to those in the tomb He has given life!' And for a Christian this is real, or it is nothing. As part of the morning and evening prayers for an ordinary Orthodox Christian living in the world one prays to one's guardian angel—who is considered to be a real presence and being. And saints are thought to be those women and men who, through imitating Christ in their lives, and through radiating Christ's love through their whole beings, have become part of Christ's body, so much so that a heavenly scent sometimes breaks through into the reality of this world through their dead bodies, through their 'relics'. And it is not only we who are astonished as readers. As Metropolitan Nikolaos discovers, God's judgment is also often something bewildering and unexpected, for a drunkard of a monk turns out, after death, to have joined Christ in heaven, for his corpse does not stink but exudes a sweet and heavenly scent.

How exactly is all this possible? What exactly is an ascetic and what on earth is asceticism, or monasticism, for that matter? What does a saint look like and what does he do and say? Can the human person go beyond what is humanly possible, what she or he is humanly capable of? Can we become more than what we are, thereby fulfilling our true nature? Can the irrationality or the non-reason of the fool be greater and more rational than human reason? All these questions, and more, are what concerns the author, and are the signposts by which he follows his spiritual quest as he walks the paths of Athos, treading the inner way of the spirit. We may be surprised, shocked even, at what he uncovers and discovers; but we may also find that a chink has opened in our selves and that light may be flooding in.

14 March 2007 Athens

Introduction

'THE MOUNT WHICH GOD DESIRED FOR HIS ABODE':[1]
A PLACE OF UNIVERSAL COORDINATES AND HEAVENLY BEARINGS

The higher one climbs, so science tell us, the weaker gravity becomes, the less we feel the pull of the earth and the looser the ties with it become, the easier it is to sever oneself from its exacting and inexorable presence, the lighter one becomes.

But the closer one feels to the heavens—which, while yet intangible, are so real, so desired. Less concrete, heaven seems more real than earth. The higher one ascends, the purer the air, the sharper one's hearing, the broader the horizon, the keener one's sense of truth. Truth seems more compelling than reality.

It is here that, for over a thousand years, and more than anywhere else in the Orthodox world, monasticism has been lived in its most unadulterated

---

[1] Ps. 68:16.

form. While the passing of the centuries may have left its secular mark; while—and it is only to be expected—there also people may have displayed their weaknesses and even their passions; while modern 'civilisation' may have done its work; yet in some inexplicable and indiscernible way Athos has not lost its blessed way of life, those unceasing and unique manifestations of grace, its rare and singular spiritual strength. It has kept its living link with divine space and time: the place of the Kingdom of God and the time of the Lord are ever near. It has weathered human error; it has withstood ill-conceived modernisation; it has worn the passing of time and people, whether emperor or everyman. In the face of human weakness one is not scandalised. In the face of even grave mistakes one does not lose hope. Its truth endures. The Holy Mountain is the most real mountain there is. At its spiritual summit one senses the absence of anything that would tie one to earth, space and time. One experiences heaven as it is found in Scripture, the world as the one, Holy, Catholic and Apostolic Church lives it, eternity as it is revealed through theology.

It is like a rock that stands at the swirl of the tide. Political influence, the highs and lows of human nature, the indiscriminate use of technology, endless tourists, quarrels, rivalry and even hatred between the monks, a narrowly parochial outlook and adversaries of all kinds: while the waves may cover it for a while or beat against it, its core remains impermeable.

There is something shielding it: perhaps it is the genuineness of its monastic life or the variety of the forms it takes; perhaps it is the way it has withstood the test of time and its treasures and splendour; perhaps it is its autonomous status and the *avaton*[2] rule forbidding women; perhaps it is its universal character; but surely it must be its protection by the Mother of God, and the particular sense of God's grace one finds there. Byzantium was a theocracy, yet it fell after eleven centuries of glory. Mount Athos is entering the fourteenth century of its existence, but to walk its paths is to tread the steps of the life of the age to come. One feels that it is a place not of this world 'where God will dwell for ever'.[3]

---

[2] A monastic principle prevailing on Mount Athos that does not allow women to enter the Athonite state and visit the monasteries. The *avaton* principle likewise may be applied to men in women's monasteries.

[3] Ps. 68: 16.

PART ONE
THE VISIBLE ATHOS

Chapter 1

CHILDHOOD VISION

E ver since I was a child I have felt a great sense of awe for the Holy Mountain, monasticism and the ascetics. Still, I was never drawn to such a life: perhaps I did not even want to contemplate the idea. No, I wasn't cut out for it; it wasn't for me. Yet anything to do with Athos and asceticism created in me a unique feeling, quite different to anything else. There were other things that filled me with wonder: the sky, the universe, science, the achievements of human genius, poetical and musical inspiration, knowledge and intelligence coupled with humility, the unassuming person of talent, natural goodness and kindness. All these things have never ceased to enthral me. But the idea of the ascetic, of the person who denies all of these things, the thought that someone can die to his nature, to look beyond knowledge, and come into eternity and into the place of God, this idea—I do not know why—seemed to me the only thing that could not come to an end, the only thing that was admirable, genuine and true. Fortunately, of course, I did not know much about the ascetic way of life, nor did I have any direct experience of it. I say 'fortunately' because I held this idealised and unprocessed image in my childish soul and, unaltered, it constantly and intensely stimulated the universe of my spiritual ideals. It is better to begin life with ideals than with experiences.

I finished primary school and went to secondary school. The images I had formed in my mind and my inner sense of wonder did not change. I remember, I was twelve years old and in my first year of secondary school. On the road, outside our house in Thessalonica, I saw two monks. It was quite a rare sight: you did not see them in the city very often then. Their rule did not allow it. I could tell they were monks by the monastic hats they wore, although it was their behaviour and whole bearing that made them stand out. They did not have the air and the ease of the priests one usually saw. Their reticent manner spoke of their sense of unease with this world. Our world. I was filled with the insatiable curiosity to look at them but I was too timid. I felt that even in my innocence I would be like a thief stealing away their hidden inner riches. I wanted to observe them, but no, it was an irreverent desire. I had to respect their need to preserve their rule of invisibility and the reason that had taken them out of their hidden mystery and brought them before my eyes. Conscious of my ignorance of their lives, I could not look, even briefly, at their faces. But I was also afraid. The wonder unconsciously turned into indefinable fear. Whatever the case, I hid. They appeared on the street, and my response was to hide from view. In the days that followed, I kept on dreaming about ascetics. And every time I was filled with an inexpressible combination of secret joy and indescribable awe.

My cousins used to spend their summers in the village of Ouranoupolis[4] and would go on frequent trips to Athos. I would listen to their vivid, if somewhat embroidered, tales of tempests, miracles, saints and mysteries. So as I grew up, and from my early adolescence, the names of particular monks and ascetics began to be etched on my memory, along with details of their lives and personalities: Fr Paisios, Fr Gerasimos of the Skete[5] of Little St Anne, Fr Gabriel of Dionysiou, Fr Ephraim and the Danielaioi Brotherhood. They also told me how my uncle would read them stories from the

---

[4] A small town on the Athos peninsula, from where boats depart for Daphne on Mount Athos itself.

[5] A small monastic settlement that is a dependency of one of the sovereign monasteries. It is made up of several autonomous huts or *kalyvia*, which are all situated near a church used for common worship called the *Kyriako*. See also footnote 12.

Gerondikon[6]. For him this book had been an important discovery and, from what I understood, it was
his great love. I never asked what it was about, but
I always wondered what on earth stories about old
men and women had to do with the holy ascetics.

---

[6] *Gerondikon*: a collection of sayings and events from the lives
of the ascetics, the desert fathers (or elders) of the East. The
word *Gerondikon* comes from the Greek word *gerondas* which
means both old man and elder, hence the confusion in the
young boy's mind.

Chapter 2

BETWEEN DREAM AND FANTASY

Wednesday, 25th August 1971, or 12th August by the old calendar.[7] It was six o'clock in the morning and we were waiting at the bus station in Thessalonica. Three friends and I were ready to take our first steps on the Mountain. There were about thirty-five passengers, of whom three or four were monks. One of them was the sweetest old man. A fine and noble figure, his face was open, peaceful and kind. His words were full of gentle good-will and he spoke an archaizing form of Greek.[8] A man enquired anxiously if the bus we had already put our things on was going to Ouranoupolis. He wanted to make sure. The old monk replied, 'That is so, my good sir. We are

---

[7] The old, Julian calendar is thirteen days behind the modern Gregorian calendar. Athos still follows the old calendar.

[8] This was *katharevousa*, a literary form of Modern Greek 'purified' of foreign elements and which contained features borrowed from Ancient Greek.

bound for the heavenly village of Ouranoupolis.'[9]

How wonderfully he put it. I looked at his hands. He was holding a parcel addressed to 'The Reverend Fr Gerasimos of Little St Anne, Hymnographer, the Skete of Little St Ann.' 'My!' I thought, 'that must be where he is going. He must know him.' I had heard a fair deal about him. Indeed, I had built up quite an impressive image of hymnographers. My mother had told me about St Romanos the Melodist, St John of Damascus and Koukouzelis. I was captivated by the thought of him: in order to be able to write and compose hymns one's heart would have to hear the divine harmony.

What a blessing—we were sitting next to each other. We fell into conversation: it turned out that the old monk was Father Gerasimos himself. I was overjoyed at this coincidence. What captivating language he used, and what an entrancing combination of solemnity and simplicity he contained in his person. I was just starting out on life, while he was in the winter of his old age. How different were our paths in life. He wrote hymns, while I preferred to solve equations. He lived in the desert, while I lived in the world. He had made

---

[9] Ouranoupolis literally means 'heavenly city' or 'town of the heavens', from *ouranos* (heaven) and *polis* (town or city).

eternity and the glory of God his aim, while I sought after earthly things, the victim of my own personal ambition.

After a journey of three-and-a-half hours along roads that twisted through the verdant Cholomonda mountain range, we reached Ouranoupolis, a small, charming little village. This was the last harbour before the 'heavenly haven' of Mount Athos. It was as enchanting as its name suggested: 'town of the heavens'.[10]

In the distance could be seen the mountain of Athos: towering, stately and commanding. I could not take my eyes off it. I could not wait until midday when the boat was to leave.

It was a glorious day. We handed over our identity cards (they would be handed back to us in Karyes together with our residence permits) and the boat sailed. Fr Gerasimos gave us a running commentary: the old customs house, the settlement of Chourmitsa, the hillside skete of Thivais, the old landing-stages, scattered cells,[11] the monasteries of Dochiariou and Xenophontos, and the Russian monastery. After two hours the port of Daphne came into view in the distance. The old, low stone buildings gave the impression of another age and time.

---

[10] See footnote 9 above.

[11] A *kellion* or cell is a separate monastic dwelling which has several rooms and a chapel.

We were nearly there. The engines were turned off. We were preparing to step on the 'untrodden' sacred ground of Mount Athos. What we had dreamed of and idealized in our minds was about to become a reality. We were about to fulfil our long-held ambition and yet we were unable to really take in what was happening.

'My disciples are waiting for me,' Fr Gerasimos said, interrupting our thoughts.

A wonderful scene ensued. Two solemn-looking monks, his disciples, were standing motionless waiting for the boat, heads bowed and eyes turned downwards. As soon as the vessel came into shore, they hurried up to him, bowed down with unmistakable respect to take his blessing, kissed his hand, and gathered up his bags and the packages. They were Fr Mitrophan and Fr Spiridon. As Fr Gerasimos bade us farewell, he invited us to come and see him at his hut.[12]

'We shall be overjoyed to receive you in our humble hut. We shall be expecting you.' His parting words were, 'May you go in peace.'

Our feet were stepping on Mount Athos. Here the past is of greater value than the living present,

---

[12] A hut (*kalyvi* in Greek) is a simple monastic dwelling for a limited number of monks under an elder, with a little property around it and a chapel attached. Several huts together form a skete.

and the future has an even greater value. The wealth of its heritage is nothing before the riches of its lived theology. Its tradition is more eloquently persuasive of an eternal prospect than reminiscent of an historical identity. The brilliance of its treasures fades into insignificance compared to the priceless contents of the reliquaries and even of the ossuaries which seem to exude more life than the monks in their cells. 'And to those in the tombs He has given life.'[13] Those who lie asleep are more awake than the 'living'. The ones who have been 'made perfect' are more real than those who are 'being made perfect'.[14] Those who have shaken off the burden of this earthly life are more truly alive than those who are still living.

In 1964 two tourists tried to steal a jasper chalice from Vatopedi Monastery. It was said that its value was estimated to be equal to the budget for that year for the state of Greece as such. A touch exaggerated, for sure. Yet Athos has a worth that cannot be calculated in monetary terms. It is measured in miracles, in acts of divine Providence, in man's ability to 'intervene' in God's will.

Daphne was relatively noisy and bustling. There were no cars, of course, apart from the old, low-ceilinged bus that was going to Karyes. There were

---

[13] From the hymn for Easter.
[14] Hebrews 12: 23.

about sixty or seventy people in all; one third of them monks, the rest laymen. With their furrowed brows, the monks wore faded habits and looked rather grubby. They were grave and hurried, unworldly, otherworldly. There was nothing sophisticated about their behaviour. Their roughness did not offend. They did not say much and they did not indulge in pleasantries.

Some people were taking the boat to the skete of St Anne or returning to Ouranoupolis, and the rest were taking the bus to Karyes. In a few minutes Daphne would be empty: the quiet hour was just beginning. Its only inhabitants were the civil servants who worked at the post office, the customs house and the police station, and the proprietors of the shops; about ten people in all. At the time when Athos plunges into the quietude of prayer and stillness, Daphne descends into the quietness of worldly inactivity, of boredom and lethargy, of the radio and backgammon.

We left Daphne to its peculiar quietness and set off for Karyes on the bus. What a strange bus it was. It could not have had more than twenty-five or thirty seats. The driver stepped into it as if he were getting onto a mule: so low was it. He turned the key in the ignition. It would not start. He kicked it angrily. The engine started up. 'Well, this low little bus really is more like an animal,' I thought.

There were no seats left and I had to stand. I was too tall to stand upright and had to keep my head bent down. I wondered whether everyone used to be under five-foot-seven. There were about ten monks on the bus. They were quiet souls, with their woven cloth bags, working their prayer-ropes in their hands, their faces free of worry, anxiety or cares. Their bearing did not reveal the depths of their personal life of prayer; what it did betray was the profundity of Athonite monastic life.

As we drove past Xeropotamou Monastery I eagerly absorbed every detail. It was an impressive building, if somewhat dilapidated. In places the vegetation had gradually begun to take over. It was a wonderful forest. Time, like a voracious wild beast, had devoured everything in its path leaving behind only bones and fragments. This was the state that half the monastery was in. It was a half-burnt ruin.

Far down below could be seen the port of Daphne. The wooded mountainside plunged abruptly into the sea and its reflection lent it a wild and uniquely beautiful green-black hue. The bus roared along the dirt road until we reached the ridge, which was called the 'cross', and then the descent began. An impressive view opened out: a whole host of hermitages, cells, domes, crosses, sketes and ruined buildings not only spread over the surrounding area of Karyes but also the whole eastern side of Athos. In the distance could be seen the Monastery of Iviron and below, at the base of the mountain, was the Monastery of Koutloumousiou. The whole of the eastern flank was densely forested. Towering chestnut trees covered the whole field of view, apart from the desert of Kapsala where bushes and pine trees predominated.

Chapter 3

A NIGHT AT KARYES

We arrived at Karyes. An atmosphere of mystery hung about the place. It was as if one was stepping into another age. Everything was old. Time had done its work, yet the spirituality of the place had acted to preserve: there were ramshackle buildings, cobbled alleyways, old street lamps, doors and windows. Outside there were a few marginal types, dirty, and forsaken by all. They had nowhere else to go. Here they were accepted and tolerated. A few quaint little shops on either side of the road, the pot plants outside the houses, and some voices that reached us from afar were reminders of what we had left behind. There was a restaurant and a shabby-looking antediluvian establishment. I caught my breath as I glimpsed three folding beds through an open window. The conditions were grimly primitive. This was not a place to stay the night: here were the perfect conditions for a sleepless night. Nevertheless everything was picturesque.

We retrieved our identity cards from the police

station. The building of the Holy Community, the 'parliament' of Athos, had altogether quite a different atmosphere. At the entrance waved the standard of a yellow and black double-headed eagle alongside the Greek flag. Everything reminded one of Byzantium. We venerated[15] the wonder-working icon of the Mother of God known as the *Axion Estin* in the Church of the Protaton;[16] and marvelled at the brilliance of the work of Panselinos.[17] The murals were full of life; everything was different. A monk, who was weary of the effort and routine but full of faith and deeply devout, gave us all the information we needed.

We set off without delay for the *kellion*[18] of the Skourtaioi Brotherhood, which entailed some walking uphill. We wanted to venerate the skull of St Nikodimos the Athonite. There we were received by a pious and excessively energetic monk. I was filled with contrition at the sight of the skull. I thought of what it had contained, and kissed it

---

[15] In the Orthodox Tradition icons are venerated and kissed. Veneration should not be confused with worship, for only God is worshipped.

[16] The Church of the Protaton is the cathedral of Karyes, famous for its wall-paintings by Panselinos.

[17] Manuel Panselinos: the main representative of the Macedonian School of fresco-painting, who lived in the 14th century.

[18] See footnote 11.

reverently. I had read about St Nikodimos and I loved him for two things: he had been intelligent and, dare I say it, extreme.

From here we walked down to the Seraphimaioi brotherhood, where we were to spend the night. Fr Chrysostom—who was from Constantinople and who was a relation of one of the friends I had gone there with—was expecting us. He was overjoyed to see us and welcomed us with great warmth. The house was old, but spotlessly clean. Inside it was well-kept, and there were pictures, antiques and ornaments. It spoke of refinement and hospitality. His cell-servant, Fr Pangraty, a quiet and taciturn young monk, brought us the traditional tray of hospitality:[19] *raki*,[20] a spoon-sweet,[21] water, and coffee. It was about 6 o'clock in the evening.

While they prepared some supper for us, we went to the Monastery of Koutloumousiou. On the way there we met a monk who was munching nuts and ambling along slowly without a care in the world. He greeted us and offered us some of the nuts. He started talking to us about Mount Athos

---

[19] My thanks are due to Graham Speake for this phrase, which he uses in his book *Mount Athos: Renewal in Paradise* (Yale, 2002).

[20] An aniseed-flavoured aperitif.

[21] Usually some kind of fruit preserved in syrup, which is served on a small plate and eaten with a teaspoon.

and immediately turned to the spiritual life. He spoke about the 'other' life after death with great feeling and at the same time with an attractive *naïveté*, as if he were talking about his fields; and about the gifts and grace of God as if he were talking about his garden. We all warmed to his exuberant and unaffected manner. He did not stop talking for a minute—he was in a world of his own. We later learnt that his name was Modestos.

We entered the monastery. We had heard that there were only seven monks. The atmosphere was bleak. I was struck by a sense of neglect and desolation. There was an earthy smell and debris scattered about. These were the only signs of life. Everything else seemed to be dead. There was no one to tell us or show us anything. Then, at the entrance, next to the tap, we came across a monk of about seventy, or perhaps younger. As soon as he saw us, he asked if we were going to become monks.

'Where? In this graveyard?' I thought to myself, gulping.

I did not answer his question. I remained stubbornly but good-naturedly silent. The others spoke about the will of God: 'If it is God's will.'

But he wanted to know what *our* will was. He turned to us again: 'It certainly is *God's* will. But is it *your* will?'

We left somewhat hastily, feeling very relieved, and arrived back at the Seraphimaioi brotherhood at about seven o'clock. The simplicity and child-like spirituality of Fr Modestos had made an impression on me. When we had asked his name he had evaded the question. We saw him again later at the feast-day of the Monastery of Iviron. It was then we learnt what he was called.

At about half-past-eight the food was ready. Night had fallen. Light was provided by paraffin lamps. It was a picturesque, fairytale scene. The table was set with fine antique tableware. The food was very good: fried aubergines, peppers, courgettes, potatoes, stuffed vine-leaves with fennel, tomato salad, garlic sauce, aubergine dip, peaches and pears. Fr Chrysostom apologized for using oil, but explained that hospitality demanded it. In any case, the oil was mainly seed-oil, he added. I did not quite understand what he meant by this. Perhaps the 'seed-oil' meant the sin was a lesser one, and the 'mainly' that the craftiness was greater. But what was certain was that the greatest thing of all was the hospitality. He was evidently sad that we had come during a period of fasting, when olive oil was not allowed. Fr Pangraty did not say anything. I warmed to his modesty and his willingness.

Even if a man of movingly great humanity, Fr

Chrysostom seemed more like a layman in a monk's habit; a pure soul, yet he was one who did not seem to have cultivated the monastic spirit. He had nothing of a spiritual nature to say. We told him that we would be going to Stavronikita Monastery: he did not really like the abbot—he was too strict; nor the brotherhood of Ephraim who lived the hesychastic[22] life in the Skete of Provata—they were too extreme. Having been assured about these clearly more genuine monks, we went off to bed.

It was 9:40 pm and everyone was asleep. I was sitting on the balcony, thinking: my first day on Mount Athos—something between a dream and fantasy. What were my first impressions? I had been struck by the unique character of its cultural landscape, yet this was not the tradition of ascetic spirituality that I had pictured in my mind since I was a child. After a while someone passed by and lit the lamps on the road. It was a layman. The street lamps were also lit with paraffin: this was a civilisation without electricity. Some voices could be heard in the post office. They soon stopped. I was still sitting on the balcony. There was total

---

[22] *Hesychia* is the practice of pure prayer and the guarding of the heart and intellect. The words hesychast, hesychasm and *hesychasterion* are all derived from the Greek word *hesychia*, which may be rendered into English in this context as 'quietude' or 'inner stillness'.

darkness. The only light came from one of the lamps, although I could not see the lamp itself. Lights twinkled in some faraway cells. Some lit up, while others went out. I assumed that some monks or hermits must be beginning or ending their rule of prayer. I felt a great sense of contrition. I sensed my inner world drawing together. The silence was total. Neither the crickets nor the cicadas could be heard. The heat was intense. I enjoyed the sound of nothing; nothing at all.

It was 10:30 pm. I was just about to go in to sleep. Suddenly, something cut through the stillness. I heard a door creak open and shut. Slow and heavy steps destroyed the sacredness of the silence but increased the sense of its depth. After a while I heard the 'glug, glug, glug' of water running through a pipe. Someone had got up to water his garden. He was right opposite. He couldn't see me, that was for certain. 'Glory to thee, O God, Glory to thee, O God,' he repeated rhythmically. My thoughts started to race and my heart began to seek some kind of response, but I declined to let it.

I went inside to go to sleep. The sheets had been freshly laundered and smelt of pure soap, and the bed was covered with a mosquito net. It was as if I had stepped into a fairy-tale. This was not the Mount Athos of my imagination. I justified everything on account of Fr Chrysostom. His hospitable disposition and the care he took over the housekeeping were truly extraordinary. Sometimes perhaps human kindness weighs more in the balance than 'spirituality'. Perhaps instinctive feelings and the spontaneous demonstrations of goodness of the natural man move us more than soundness of faith. We often see warmth and kindness as a weakness or as something offensive, yet they often speak to our heart more than an uncompromising exactitude or unwillingness to yield. I had not been looking to find characters like Fr Chrysostom on Mount Athos, nor had I wanted to. Even if I was taken aback, I recall our meeting as one of the most genuine and real encounters of my time on Athos.

And there was evening and there was morning, the first day.[23]

---

[23] Gen. 1: 5.

Chapter 4

AT FR PAISIOS'S HUT

It was Thursday 13th August, two days before the feast of the Dormition. I woke up at 6 o'clock. It was a heavy day, cloudy, hot and humid. A generous breakfast awaited us: tea, coffee, bread, jam, honey and preserved cherries in syrup. They gave us whatever they had in their cupboards. I was overwhelmed by feelings of warmth and gratitude for the love they showed us. We took Fr Chrysostom's blessing and set off at half past nine, his Abrahamic hospitality embedded in our memories. I felt moved but I had not found spiritual rest. I had been expecting something else.

The sky had cleared slightly. You could dimly make out the sun and the atmosphere was hazy. We were walking towards Fr Paisios's hut. I eagerly soaked in our surroundings. My mind was working non-stop. Today we would see what we had only imagined up until now. Lord! What sweetness I felt at this desire to behold a genuine ascetic. We had been walking for three-quarters-of-an-hour. It was not far now. I desperately wanted to see him, but I did not want to imitate his life. It was something only there to admire, not for me to do myself. I refused to accept it even as an inkling of a possibility. No, it was impossible. I was going to become a scientist. I wanted to conquer this life, the one I could see. And as for the other life, God knows.

After a little while the humble hut of Fr Paisios came into view. It was about fifteen minutes away now. The roof was made of sheet metal. A magnificent cypress tree stood right next to it. The hut was low lying. Yet it could have been the highest place on earth. As we descended the path on foot we ascended it in our soul. Nobody said anything. It was as if we were anticipating something sacred. Here there was total quietude, even if one could hear the singing of the birds, the cicadas and the rustle of the leaves. The quietude was not only strange or unusual, but it gave rise to a deep sense of mystery. It did not provoke one to enjoyment, but it created a feeling of compunction. It did not make you want to rest but to be watchful. You fell silent and everything within worked intensely as never before. You felt anguish, yet strangely serene. You were filled with anticipation. No, the quietude here was something completely different to the quietness of Karyes after the sun has set, and it was a world away from the silence of Daphne after the bus has left. In the silence of those places you hear nothing. But this quietude gives birth to new sounds; it brings you messages and melodies from the other world. In this quietude you hear the beating of your heart; you fathom the depths of your being; you perceive His depths; you hear that which 'no ear heard', and 'inexpressible words'.[24] Something can be heard here that cannot be heard anywhere else.

There it was. We were finally standing outside the entrance to Fr Paisios's hut, the Hermitage of the Holy Cross. I was gripped by fear. That's what I felt most of all: an indefinable fear; an unacknowledged and unexpressed sense of awe and wonder. We knocked on the courtyard gate cautiously, if somewhat insistently. A piece of iron served its purpose much better than any modern electric bell. Five minutes went by. There was no answer. He might not open the door—that would be the most likely scenario, they had said—he usually did not interrupt his conversation with God. But still we hoped. We conferred in whispers—we did not dare speak louder than was necessary. We decided not to knock again. The first knock must have been heard in the imposing silence. To knock again would be to shatter it with an expression of our egoism and impatience. The elder must be

---

[24] 1 Cor. 2: 9 and 2 Cor. 12: 4.

praying, for he prayed constantly. The rapping on the gate was not for him: he could hear it alright. It was for us to beg before he responded; not to receive without the humility of asking. We elected to wait. Another five minutes went by.

Just as soon as we had made up our minds to knock again, we heard the noise of a door opening. A figure appeared. He had been hiding. He now appeared before us, revealing his presence. 'Glory to thee, O God,' his voice rang out in my ears. 'Glory to thee, O God,' my heart began to respond. *He has opened the door*, I said to myself with relief, and not without a certain trepidation. He walked slowly and steadily towards us without saying anything and opened the gate.

He rarely spoke. To our greeting of 'Your blessing', he answered, in a faint voice that trembled with compunction, 'May the Lord bless you. Come in.'

I cast a fleeting glance at him. I did not dare to look again, nor could I bear it. My heart beat rapidly. I was curious, for I wanted to discover the mystery of his holiness. I was frightened, for he might find out the secret of my sinfulness. He concealed the depths of his heart out of humility, and I did so out of egoism.

We entered his modest hut. All the dimensions were small. The doors were low and narrow. The ceiling was low. Even the geometric dimensions were humble here. We went through to his chapel. There was a simple iconostasis constructed out of wooden boards. The paper icons were of the Russian westernized type. They had no wooden backs and so they could be easily torn, for they had been fixed straight onto the boards with nails and drawing pins. Here one found only that which was necessary, and everything was at its physical limits. As we venerated the icons Father Paisios intoned slowly and emphatically, 'Glory to thee, O God' and, 'Lord, have mercy.'

What struck me was that, while the hands of the saints had worn away on nearly all the icons, on the icon of Christ it was His feet. It was on another, later, occasion that I took the opportunity to ask him why. It was then that he told me, the tears streaming down:

'We kiss the face with love, the hands out of respect and the feet out of contrition only. We do not kiss God on His face, when we can kiss His feet. We may dare to kiss the hands of the saints but we can only bear to kiss Christ on His feet.'

Outside the hut was the grave of Father Tychon, who had been Father Paisios's elder and who had died three years earlier. There were a couple of rosemary bushes, a grapevine and the tall cypress tree—it lifted your soul up to heaven just to behold.

We went into his guest sitting-room: it could not
have been any bigger than six foot by eight. A natural protrusion at the base of the wall, covered by a
brown army blanket, served as a sofa. He brought
us some water and Turkish delight. We waited for
him to say something but he remained silent. His
head bowed, he calmly sat making a prayer-rope.
Finally someone broke the silence. I do not recall
exactly what he asked. I remember only how the
elder, in his faltering voice, described first the love
of God, and how the sense of it gives birth to our
love for Him. How beautifully he described it all.
He spoke to us of the sweetness of God's gifts, the
sunlight of His presence, the nobleness of the
saints, the manliness of the martyrs, and of our own
philotimo[25] or responsive gratitude.

In a similar tone and rhythm he described the
splendour of prayer as the sense of God's presence
and the movement of our own love towards Him. I
just sat and listened. I soaked in as much as I could
with my eyes, ears and mind. I was more interested
in what lay beyond his speech and outward appearance. His eyes and face spoke more than his words.

---

[25] *Philotimo* is a Greek word which Father Paisios used very
often; it is our gratitude towards God and our fellow men, and
the spiritual sensitivity which we demonstrate in trying to repay
the slightest good that other people do us. In other words, it
means 'responsive gratitude'.

They gave away what he tried to conceal from us. Questions were asked more for the sake of it than anything else. I remained silent, resolving to come back with a list of questions. I thirsted for anything beyond the average, the conventional and the ethically 'correct'. I had become weary of ready-made answers in respect of the spiritual life. But Father Paisios spoke with a new and original voice, and one hung on his every word. He heard the 'things that cannot be told' as he trod the path of inner quietude. But within his invisibility he revealed the grace of God.

Here you could hear the things that cannot be told and see the things that cannot be seen. Every hermitage is like a deep well. Physicists tell us that from the bottom of a well you can see the stars at midday. The walls of the well absorb the sunbeams reflected upon them, and the hermitage absorbs every sound, image or worldly care, allowing the ascetic to hear, see and think clearly without being distracted.

Time was getting on and, very politely and gently, he gave us to understand that we should be getting on our way. We were already running late. We went out into the courtyard. He went back in to bring us each a prayer-rope that he had knotted himself. It was his gift of blessing. In the hollow of a tree standing beside us I spied a glass jar containing hazelnuts. The word 'blessing' was written on the jar. Everything here is offered as a blessing, I thought. He came with us a little way to show us a shortcut. We each took his blessing and set off.

My mind was bombarded with thoughts. Maybe we had gone to see him out of curiosity and not out of spiritual thirst? Perhaps, after all, he had been wasting his time with us? The value of his time was 'measured' in terms of our spiritual understanding. I turned back to catch a glimpse of him, even of his back. He had disappeared. He was impatient to get back to his life of prayer.

I went to see Father Paisios on another occasion in 1976, this time with one of my friends from university. I remember how charmingly and sweetly he expressed everything.

'Young men, what are you studying?' he asked us.

'Physics,' we answered.

'So you are both physicists? Well, then. You must learn the physics of metaphysics. If you know about the splitting of the atom, then you must learn about the spiritual splitting of the individual. When we come to know ourselves and reach a state of self-knowledge, then that is when the splitting of our individuality takes place. If we do not humble ourselves so that the atom of our own individuality can be split, then the spiritual energy that is needed to overcome the gravity of our nature won't be released. Only in that way, my good young people, will we be able to trace our spiritual orbit.'

What a wonderful surprise. He spoke our language in his language.

'Spiritual life is easy,' he said. 'My yoke is easy and my burden is light,'[26] Christ tells us.

'But "the gate is narrow and the way is hard",'[27] my friend replied amiably.

'Fatty flesh, my blessed one, makes it narrow. Get rid of that and you will see how easy it is.'

Our love must be the same towards everyone. Only then is it God's love. If we love some people more than others, we must suspect that egotism has crept in.

The more we forget ourselves, the more we see the blessings of God in our life. And what does God in His loving-kindness not give us? (How warmly and sweetly he pronounced the word 'loving-kindness'!) At times we feel our bones bending like wax, unable to bear the weight of His gifts. Under the love of God everything buckles. Beside it, everything melts.

He spoke to us of the marvels of prayer and God's grace. He told us how he had met a monk who, in simplicity of heart and, taking literally

---

[26] Matt. 11: 30.

[27] Matt. 7: 14.

Christ's words that he had given his disciples the power 'to tread on snakes and scorpions',[28] had picked up poisonous snakes without any fear and thrown them out of his garden. There was another monk who, as he prayed, would be taken by the grace of God to far-flung realms, and there perform miracles and reveal the power of God, and then be brought back. Once the same monk had woken up and had found himself holding a flower that grows only by the Caspian Sea. That is where God had taken him.

With all this the elder broke the shell of our rationalism. He gave us intimations of another kind of way of life and thinking. Yet there was one idea he did not succeed in planting in my mind—that of my vocation. I stubbornly refused to look in that direction…

Twelve years later, in 1988, I found myself on Athos once more as a novice, this time with my vocation as an ally. It had been a very dry summer. For months there had not been a drop of rain. The springs and streams had stopped flowing: the water sources had dried up. No one was able to grow any-thing. No tomato plant grew above three feet high. They made a pitiful sight as they hung from their canes like consumptives. The pepper, courgette and

---

[28] Luke 10: 19.

cucumber plants were the same or even worse.

Fr Paisios's garden was the exception. He did not grow all kinds of vegetable; only those that did not need to be cooked, for his ascetic rule did not allow for it. He had planted nine tomato plants and one cucumber. That year his unwatered tomato plants stood more than six-and-a-half foot high: what they lacked in water they made up for in height. And as for the tomatoes, they were the size of small melons. I was filled with amazement at this miraculous sight. The living water of divine grace replaced the need for natural water.

Armed with the smallest amount of water and our great hope in God, we are able to provoke Him spiritually, and He transfigures nature. The more the logic of this world and the weightiness of earthliness contract within us, the more vital and true the appearance of God becomes in the 'atmosphere' of our soul and in the 'environment' of our life.

Jokingly he put me in between the tomatoes, exclaiming, 'What a shame, and I thought you were tall. Here even my tomato plants are taller than you. Just think if I had watered them!'

All the cells in the whole surrounding area benefited from Fr Paisios's tomato plants. In the end I do not know if we kept going with just tomatoes, although what I do know is that we tasted God's blessings.

He who wanted little, enjoyed much. How can someone forget such an experience? Such experiences irrigate even the most unwatered souls among the Athonite monks and, in our arid times, cause them to produce in a miraculous manner the most succulent spiritual fruits of our times. 'Their faith and life sustain the universe.'[29]

He often used to tell me how, when God visits the heart, man becomes so subtle and gentle in his relation with nature, that he no longer disturbs it, nor needs to protect himself: he does not tread on flowers or nettles, kill ants or brush off flies, but he shows respect for the broken twig, the fruitless tree, the annoying insect, the aggressive animal. When you come across a wild animal or a snake, if you love it in this way it will not harm you: for it loves you also. You become a friend of nature, and all creation returns the love and trust. You show respect for it in its sighing and in its weakness, you water it with prayer and it responds by producing marvellous fruits. The harvest you reap is not the result of the laws of cause and effect, but is a form of divine blessing. In this way the environment is transformed into a holy place and natural laws are replaced by miracles and acts of divine interven-

---

[29] Sunday of Orthodoxy, Synodal Statement of the 7th Ecumenical Council (787).

tion. This is ascetic ecology.

In 1988, Father Paisios and his garden bore out the sweet-sounding words and teachings I had heard in 1976 and reinforced the deep and lasting impression he had made on my soul during that blessed meeting in 1971. I remember, then, how I had not needed even to look at him or even to hear him speak. It had been enough just to feel that I was in the presence of a 'transcendental' person, that I had met an ascetic, a living saint.

Chapter 5

STAVRONIKITA MONASTERY AND THE FEAST-DAY OF IVIRON MONASTERY

My visit to Fr Paisios's hut in 1971 is one of the most important experiences of my life. I might not have opened my mouth to say anything, but my heart opened. It was there that the first crack appeared. I might have felt that all my feelings and thoughts were jumbled up inside me, but as soon as I left I sensed for the first time a little order entering my inner world. The experience not only confirmed my every imagining—it surpassed it.

We left the hermitage and arrived at the Monastery of Stavronikita at about 12 noon. It was a pure jewel. Built straight onto the rock, it stood right next to the sea. At the entrance a magnificent vine was there to greet us. We were struck by the monumental silence. A monk was working in the garden. We could hear two other monks talking in low tones, but we could not tell where they were. After a while the guest-master, Fr Theodosios, arrived. A gaunt figure, his words were measured and his movements restrained and precise. Some monks passed by. They seemed to have a spiritual profundity and to have cultivated the monastic spirit: they did not look about or talk needlessly. We went to the guest house. Everything was all very clean. It was a wonderful day and the view was spectacular: to the North stood the Monastery of Pantokrator, that also clung onto a rocky outcrop. In the opposite direction the whole mountainous bulk of Athos opened out. To the East lay the sea and the island of Thasos appearing crystal clear on the horizon. Further south one could make out the silhouette of Lemnos.

The Abbot, Fr Basil, was not at Vespers. He was away in Karyes. Fr Gregory was there, the second in order of seniority at the monastery. He was solemn and gracious, and you did not feel very free in his presence. His hands were covered in calluses from making prostrations. Here too light was provided by paraffin lamps.

I had no balcony to sit and muse in the evening, so I went straight to sleep. Besides, here we would be getting up for church at 3 o'clock in the morning. The service had a very penitential atmosphere, although the chanting was not terribly good. The food was simple and the garden was carefully tended. There were fifteen monks at the most. This entrancingly beautiful place had a genuinely monastic feel. It was clearly a well-disciplined cenobitic monastery.[30]

It was the eve of the feast of the Dormition of the Mother of God, Friday, 14th August 1971 by the old calendar. We were getting ready to go to the monastery of Iviron for the feast-day there. We set off at about eleven a.m. After a while the bus made a short stop. Facing us in the distance rose the majestic mountain of Athos. It was like a good father embracing his children: its twenty monasteries, twelve sketes and innumerable cells; and its one thousand and two hundred monks. The gulf of Athos is home to a thousand-year-old tradition; here an army of saints finds repose, a multitude of holy relics and a unique collection of rare artifacts are kept; and man finds a safe sanctuary in the midst of his sighing and desire for God. Here ascetics toil and weep, but God finds rest. Somewhere amongst it all was me. I was on my 'tour'. I was satisfying my curiosity.

I thought about all this so much that my head

---

[30] A monastery in which the abbot is elected for life and to whom all monks owe absolute obedience. In the cenobium none of the monks is permitted to own personal property, and they hold all things in common. Services are held in the main monastery church or *Katholikon*, and all meals are taken together in the common refectory.

nearly burst. I felt so much that my heart nearly gave way. I was deeply moved. Yet—and how strange it was—my will was not touched or affected. So easily did I slip into forgetfulness. I did not know how it was possible: it was as if all these things were drawing towards me and I was moving away. What an inexplicable mystery the human person is!

We arrived at Iviron Monastery and were put in a room for twelve people. We had got here early enough to find a bed and secure our corner. A huge number of visitors had begun to arrive by boat, mule and bus, and on foot. Where had they all come from so suddenly? There might have been five hundred people. Many of them were ailing and infirm. A hundred or more were monks. Everyone was here to venerate the icon of the Mother of God, called 'Our Lady of the Gate'.[31] The Vigil service started at 9 pm. Bishop Epiphanios of Paros and Naxos was officiating. It was an impressive sight. There were many unusual liturgical practices: the chandeliers were swung at certain points and the first words of the hymns were intoned by a soloist before the entrance of the choir. Two deacons held the huge

---

[31] A miracle-working icon of the Mother of God, in Greek called *Portaitissa*, which is kept in the Monastery of Iviron and which is considered one of the most important holy icons on the Holy Mountain. Literally, *Portaitissa* means the 'door-keeper'.

Gospel book, which they said weighed thirty-one kilos. The chanters were from the Danielaioi and Thomades Brotherhoods. One had the sense of real rejoicing. Some sprightly old monks hurried incessantly back and forth as they carried out various duties, unaffected joy and a genuine sense of solemnity written on their faces. The Divine Liturgy was full of majesty. The Bishop was robed with the Episcopal vestments in the centre of the church. I was impressed by the unique spectacle of all this Byzantine magnificence.

What can I say of the *kolyva*,[32] the wheat of memorial? Some monks who were iconographers spent all night creating a picture of the Mother of God out of coloured sugar on top of the most delicious *kolyva* I have ever tasted. The final result was a masterpiece. I had never seen anything like it. I wondered how, at the end of the meal after the vigil service, the bishop could, with one movement of the spoon, destroy this unrepeatable work of art that they had worked on all night long.

The service finished at about midday and, before the concluding words of dismissal,[33] we went down

---

[32] Boiled wheat mixed with sugar, sesame seeds and dried nuts offered at memorial services. The top is covered with sugar and is often decorated.

[33] The concluding words of services in the Greek Orthodox Tradition are usually 'Through the prayers of our holy Fathers,

to the refectory for the feast: fish soup, snails, tomato salad, grapes and pudding. My eyes remained fixed on the monks. I was more interested in what was going on around me than in the food.

After the bishop, the most important person there was the former Abbot[34] of the Great Lavra. As he entered the refectory, I noticed that he had two large holes in the heels of his socks. These holes were only slightly smaller than the great many stains that adorned his habit like military medals. His appearance was certainly the one thing that he was not concerned about.

The abbot of another monastery grabbed his bowl, brought it to his mouth and slurped up his soup, just like little children in respectable families do to annoy their mothers. He was sitting together with the bishop, the civil governor and the other officials. They did not pass comment nor did they seem to mind.

I had never done anything like that, nor could I. I could never wear socks with holes, nor slurp my soup in front of others. Yet I was terribly envious.

Lord Jesus Christ, have mercy on us, and save us.' Orthodox Services are often very long, although this is because several services are held in succession, and thus appear to be one single service.

[34] The Greek word is *prohegumen*, a former abbot who has either resigned or has been replaced.

They were simple people, carefree and unaffected; indifferent to worldly convention and its pointless misunderstandings; blessed and free. May God forgive them. I was at the height of my youthful doubting, and seeing them made me realize that man should not look well-behaved, but should behave the way he is. And as for all this blessed anarchism: what an amazing place Athos was. On the feast-day of the monastery the abbots did what most young people cannot do in their rebellious years.

At the end of the meal I met the monks of the Danielaioi brotherhood: Fr Daniel, Fr Gregory and Fr Stephen. Sincere, friendly and welcoming, their clear eyes were full of warmth. It was as if they had known us for years. They invited us to their *kellion* at Katounakia. I had heard about them and was thrilled at the idea. We all left for Daphne on Sunday 16 August, 1971: they in the Civil Governor's jeep and we in the police car.

Chapter 6

KATOUNAKIA AND THE DANIELAIOI BROTHERHOOD

We took the boat that was going to Katounakia. It was a beautiful, balmy summer's day. The very first thing to emerge into view was the Monastery of Simonopetra. It was an unbelievably impressive sight. Then came the Monasteries of Grigoriou, Dionysiou, St Paul, New Skete and the Skete of St Anne. For the first time well-known names now opened out before my eyes like a series of pictures. I soaked up everything—images, sounds and impressions—with my whole being.

The boat rounded the headland and at once the imposing sight of Karoulia appeared. The hermitages clinging precariously to the precipitous rock-face spoke of those bold and heroic ascetics who themselves cleave to the rock of the grace of God. I was seized by a feeling of indescribable awe. In denying their nature, these real heroes comprehend their souls. Yet in exercising violence on their nature, they understand God, and they 'constrain'

God through their way of life to listen to their prayer. Here human beings manage not to be human beings: they remain so according to their natural identity, but not according to their capabilities and way of living and being. Here even the angels cannot but feel envy and surprise. Yes, this is where God obeys man!

We got out at the jetty, walked up the steep cobbled street that led to the Danielaioi Brotherhood, and gradually cut across Karoulia to reach Katounakia. It was a wild and disconsolate place: only rocks, a sprinkling of earth and sparse scrub. A few prickly pears and almond trees scattered here and there were the only signs of life. The only living things that can survive here are those heroic ascetics who, overcoming their human nature, live constantly according to the laws and conditions of the supra-natural state. Whatever needs the sanction of nature cannot endure it here. The creature dominated by instinct moves away and disappears. The man dominated by reason moves even further away. Only those rational beings who have left behind the narrowness of their reason can live, can withstand nature, can endure their own nature, and partake of the nature of God. As we walked up the steep path on this sweltering August afternoon, wondering when it would ever come to an end, our thoughts quickly turned to the lives of these ascetics. They had chosen the unending uphill struggle in the scorching heat of the ascetic life. What they experienced every day and every moment—or as far as we were able to imagine it—we could not bear to think about even for a few minutes.

After about forty minutes we arrived at the welcome oasis of the Danielaioi. I reckoned that it must have been at an altitude of about nine hundred feet. A luxuriant vine grew at the entrance. We were shown great hospitality: *raki*, coffee, and sweets. We belong here, I thought, with a heavy heart. The thought had barely formed in my mind when a kindly and gentle old monk, Fr Niphon, asked me if I had come there to become a monk.

'No', was my immediate inner reaction, 'I don't belong here either.'

He asked me again. I remained elusive and defensive, and smiled awkwardly, unable to respond in any other way.

They were an admirable community. At that time there were eight monks: with their deep bass voices they were considered to be some of the best chanters on Athos. They numbered some of the finest icon-painters and they were justifiably renowned for their hospitality: simple, kind-hearted and warm, they seemed unaffected and genuine.

Although quite rocky and arid, the landscape was serene. In the distance could be seen the humble hermitage of St John the Forerunner that formed part of the skete of Little St Anne. This was where Fr Gerasimos of Little St Anne wrote his services and his hymns. On the opposite side was the gorge of Katounakia.

Fr Niphon took our cause to heart. He did not stop pressurizing us to become monks. My 'outer' self found it quite annoying, and my 'spiritual' self did not seem to notice. He suggested that we should find a good spiritual father in Thessalonica, who would make us see sense. He must be the kind that 'fishes' for monks, I thought, and tried to change the subject.

On Sunday afternoon Prince Michael of Romania arrived together with six others, most of whom were foreigners who did not speak Greek. A fine man, he was relatively young and had some connection with Fr Gerontios. With a complete lack of affectation they sat down with us to eat the meal of spaghetti with tomato sauce. What impressed me was that the presence of the prince did not cause the monks to make any changes in their programme. They were full of generous hospitality and did not betray any worldly superficiality or hypocrisy.

Chapter 7

KAROULIA:
VIEW OF THE INVISIBLE

Monday dawned. A young dentist whom we had met on the boat arrived and persuaded us to go to Karoulia to visit the cell of a holy ascetic, Fr Gabriel, who had fallen asleep in the Lord two years earlier.

We set off for Karoulia at about 9 o'clock in the morning; we were six in all. Ripples stirred once more across my secret inner world. In its purely visual aspect the landscape created in me a profound sense of awe simply to behold. No, I did not want to remain human. I was drawn by the thought of people who experience heaven and who live in an angelic state; it seemed to me the only truth. Everything else was not less or more true or a lesser or greater falsehood. It was a huge lie, an incredible deception and unforgivable delusion. In those places where the world is renounced, the living and vital truth shines through in all its allure and magnificence. We had reached the crucial point. The gradient was about 75–80 degrees. There—suspended and clinging to the rock—was the rectangular-shaped eyrie of that heavenly person. A monk's cloth cap and a tattered habit were the last firm evidence that this inhuman dwelling was once the home of a man; that its heroic inhabitant was in the end still a human being.

I soon realized that the intensity and rhythm of my heartbeat had increased. It was not the height that dizzied me, nor the sense of danger I felt at my every step. It was the thought of that man. My wonder surpassed the limits of my mental endurance. I looked at this threadbare garment and I venerated it. So also were his dreams, his life and his nature torn to shreds and did he hang them on the nail of divine hope. I thought how he had lived and my eyes filled with tears. I thought how he *lives* and I prayed, 'O holy one, pray to God for me.'

Just below us, about 100 metres down, was another hermitage. Someone lived there: we could see him—he had emerged from his hiding place. Scattered to the left and right were a few other buildings and ruins. I suddenly felt the intense desire to see them. We all decided to go.

We did not know the way exactly. But from the hermitage of Fr Gabriel we could make out a somewhat easier-looking route and we set off. On the way we met three others who had not made it. To our right we caught sight of some chains. We imagined that this must be 'Karoulia thoroughfare'. And indeed, slipping along amongst the big stones and prickly pears and holding tightly on to the chains that were attached to the rocks, we came to a relatively level point from where we could go in three directions. This was their...Picadilly Circus.

First of all we went to Fr Seraphim, the Russian. He looked at us with the innocent eyes of a tame wild beast—eyes that were rarely used: these people begin to see when they have their eyes closed. The sea was not visible from his cell. It was surrounded on all sides by red rocks in the shape of the Greek letter *pi*. The rock formation created a natural cave and a level space not more than fifteen square metres in area. Ascetics of old had turned this into a hermitage. The cave served as a chapel and the area in front was the cell, for sleeping, cooking and receiving guests. It was relatively dirty and untidy. It was full of icons that were mostly Russian. He did not have any refreshment to offer us. There were nine of us and we only just fitted into the 'available' space. That was what he had to offer. As you came out of the hut, the only escape was the sky. It was closed in on all sides by the rocks. To the north was a remarkable rock configuration of an upright oval boulder with an opening in the centre. I asked the monk if I could take a photograph of him standing in front of it.

'Me ruin photo,' he objected.

I pleaded with him and he gave in. The photograph was not ruined: if it revealed something of the life of a heroic ascetic, it said much about the superficiality of a naïve pilgrim. To the right, looking towards the sea, we could see a small hut built onto the sheer rock face. What was strange was that there was also a small courtyard with an almond tree. The problem was the approach: it was really quite dangerous. For about fifty metres one had to tread on particular rocks that were just wide enough to get a foothold. That was where Fr Arsenios the book-binder lived. He could not have been more than fifty years old. He was unsmiling, curt and a little abrupt, and not one to exchange the usual pleasantries. We went to see him three at a time. There was not room for any more than that. He described his work to us. Then, without saying anything, he gave us to understand that we should be on our way, and so we set off in the direction of the main part of Karoulia.

There was a twinned hut, rusty red in colour, which had been built in the recess of a sheer rock face, about twenty metres above the sea. From here a basket would be lowered on a pulley and fishermen would place dried rusks or whatever else they had for the ascetics, receiving in return items of their handiwork. This was the famous *karouli* (or pulley) from which the whole area had acquired its name. It was where Fr Pachomios lived. One of our company had a camera hanging over his shoulder. Fr Pachomios told him in no uncertain terms that he must not use it. He was visibly upset at the presence of a boat full of women tourists that had come quite close to shore. The tourist guide was describing through the microphone, 'the majesty of these heroes of the spirit who have renounced the vanity of worldly things and who are granted unique experiences and rare visions'. Certainly there could not be greater sacrilege than this in Karoulia than the ostentatious pompousness of this harsh and rough voice booming out the most vacuous and ridiculous things one could imagine. Fortunately, the vessel left quickly.

Fr Pachomios spoke briefly and frankly, mostly about the Orthodox faith and ecumenism. He was solemn, and there was no superfluity to his speech, bearing and being. His clothes were in rags. There was just enough to support life in his surroundings. It was movingly bare, and everything was old and broken: here was poverty and material decay at its height. He went to offer us something but all he had was six raisins, and we were nine. He put them onto the lid of a jar—his tray. Three of us did not get one and were given water instead. He had some rainwater in a bucket that he gave us to drink. At first we refused as we would have left him without. But he insisted. A jar served as a glass—the same for everyone. Those who had had a raisin took one sip; the others took two. We did not want to drink up all the water for here it was of very great value. We wanted to know what handiwork he produced, and he showed us three wooden combs and a few paper knives. We asked how much they were but he did not know. We took them and put down two hundred drachmas. He objected: it seemed too much. Now it was our turn to insist, and he humbly acquiesced. We asked for his blessing and left.

Upon leaving his hermitage, we had to go through eastern Karoulia, which was more accessible. Here were the hermitages we had seen on the way up to the Danielaioi Brotherhood from Katounakia landing-stage. The approach was extremely dangerous. As soon as we left Fr Pachomios's we found two wooden ladders that were nailed to the cliff at an angle of about 60 degrees. At this point the rock formed a natural protrusion that was about half a metre wide, to which the ladders were attached with thick strips of metal that also served as steps. To the left of the rock, running alongside the ladder and about a metre above it were some thick chains for handles. To the right was the sea—a drop of about thirty metres.

One by one we very carefully crossed this very

peculiar path, the 'highway' of Karoulia. It must be the only one of its kind. The ladder ran for about thirty metres, after which it became a more normal path, which led straight into a natural cave full of skeletons, skulls and bones. It was a fearful sight, but also a relief: it is better to see the skulls of others than to imagine your own. I had literally been scared out of my wits. The bones must have been those of former ascetics.

After a few minutes we found ourselves outside a hut that was fairly conventional in comparison with the others. We knocked apprehensively on the door and waited a little while. Steps could be heard. The door opened and an unusual figure emerged. His hair hung loose about his shoulders. His eyes were shining, reddish and sunken. A real skeleton with protruding cheekbones, his teeth were eaten up by disuse. Open to the throat, his habit was tied round his waist with a piece of rope, and hung off his dried-out body. The life of St Eusebius came to mind: 'his belt could not be supported around his waist for even his belly muscles had been consumed.' He looked quite dirty and he reacted with a certain degree of awkwardness. We did not know what to do or say. He made it easier for us:

'Are you Orthodox or new-calendarists?'[35]

---

[35] Old Calendarists still follow the 'old' Julian calendar, not the

The oldest person in our party answered hastily:
"Orthodo…" and faltered. He had suddenly realized what was afoot. Another awkward silence followed.

A torrent of anti-ecumenical arguments, the proclamation of dangers and exhortations to awakening and struggle ensued. We listened with heads bowed. Fortunately, we were not required to say anything: we were not called upon to do so; nor were we given the chance. We thanked him and left. It was Fr Bartholomew. Most probably the teacher of zealotism[36] in Karoulia.

As we were leaving, a very sweet-natured but rather naïve monk, Fr Mark, who had previously suggested we should go to see Fr Bartholomew, invited us into his hermitage. It was late, and so he brought some Turkish delight outside to us—small pieces that were as old as the hills and as hard as pebbles. Instead of icing sugar they must have been

---

'new' Gregorian calendar that was adopted by the Orthodox Church of Greece in 1924, and they are not in communion with the rest of Athos, the Church of Greece or the Patriarchate of Constantinople. A confusion arises, since Athos follows the old calendar, but it is not Old Calendarist.

[36] Zealots are Old Calendarists who do not commemorate the name of the Ecumenical Patriarch of Constantinople in services. They are also usually much more conservative and narrow in their outlook.

covered in dust and instead of the usual flavour they tasted of earth. Yet it was offered with great love and simplicity. Perhaps that was why it tasted so good.

Chapter 8

AT FR EPHRAIM'S HUT

B ack at the Danielaioi Brotherhood, Fr
Niphon insisted that we should go and see
a holy ascetic by the name of Fr Ephraim. He would
tell us if we should become monks. There he went
again.

'Oh no. He wants to drive us into the big net,' I
thought, 'and to send us to a man who is "saintly",
for he makes people become monks.'

I was beginning to feel ill at ease. But I was still
open to the idea of going.

At about 3 o'clock we made up our minds to go
and see Fr Ephraim. I was very afraid. It suddenly
occurred to me that he might keep me there and that
I might not be able to get away. That's how little of
an idea I had about things.

The gorge of Katounakia is one of the most
suitable places on Mount Athos for living the
ascetic life. It is a real desert. It is like a rock that
has been split in two, with only a hint of vegetation
on either side. The silence is extraordinary.
Occasionally a few wild birds shoot through the air

and dive down suddenly into naturally formed nesting places. It is full of such places: dwelling-places for birds, for wild animals, for men; for every wild person, for every holy person.

As we walked down between the rocks and sparse vegetation, in the distance we could hear a banging sound. Someone was at work. It must be a hammer. And sure enough we soon came across the man at his hut. It was Fr Gideon. He was hammering round the top of an opened tin to turn in the sharp edges. Perhaps he wanted it for a cup, although we never found out. We asked him if this was the right way to Fr Ephraim's. Having been reassured that it was we continued on our way.

As we descended into the gorge we could also hear some loud voices. Someone had to be shouting very loudly. The continual echo prevented us from making out the words, but we could hear the voices getting louder and louder, as if some people were quarrelling. So they have arguments in the 'sanctuary' of Katounakia too, I thought. As I carried on walking I could barely contain my curiosity.

We reached the next hut. The voices were coming from here. We knocked on the door. Out came a giant of a man with a radiant expression. An ascetic of about sixty years old, his eyes had the piercing gleam of diamonds. I had never seen some-one who looked at you with such a harmonious

combination of purity of soul, genuineness, austerity and sweetness. It had to be Fr Ephraim. We
asked if it really was him.

'What do you want with him?' he asked gruffly.
'Sit down for a while and I'll be back.'

There was no politeness, conventionality or
superficiality to his speech. Rather it was measured
and restrained, and marked by a sense of gravity
and inner pain.

We sat down in the courtyard, if that was the
right name for the small space in front of the door
of his hut. Inside he carried on speaking in a loud
voice. He must be talking to someone who was fairly deaf. They were not arguing. Here also was
astounding poverty. There was a heavenly quietude
and a sense of solitude. Everything was old, small
and narrow. There was nothing of worldly value.
Everything spoke of the renunciation of falsehood
and deception. After a few minutes this 'giant' came
and sat down next to us on a small stool. The sun
was shining directly into his face. He did not react
at all. He apologized for the shouting. He told us
that his elder was a hundred and five and that he
was deaf. He had been trying to get him to eat
something and to lie down.

'A sixty-year old disciple', I thought. He must
have been about that old.

I presumed that this must be Fr Ephraim. But I

did not have the courage to ask him again.

'What is your aim in life, young men? What do you do?' he asked.

'Oh no, here we go again,' I thought.

'I want to become a doctor,' my friend answered,

'A doctor?' said Fr Ephraim fiercely and rather startled. He shook his head and turned to me:

'And do you want to become a doctor too?'

'No,' I answered, 'a physicist'.

'What is all this? One of you wants to become a doctor, the other a scientist. But what is your aim in life? Do you know how to pray? Have you come to love God? Do you want to truly *live*? Do you realize that you are eternal?'

Profound questions that fell with sharp thuds onto the soft folds of our untested personalities. He had before him two 'good' young people who, even though they had been living a Christian life for years, had never managed, or at least wanted, to taste the sweetness of divine truth. We fell silent for a while. He fell silent also.

'Why do you want to be a doctor?' he asked again.

'To be useful to society,' my friend answered naively.

He winced noticeably and shook his head, unsurprisingly refusing to swallow this unconscious falsehood.

'Perhaps you want to help others too?' he asked me inquiringly and slightly perplexed.

'I like physics,' I said softly.

What were we saying? How did these words come out of our mouths? This was a hero of unfailing self-sacrifice and self-offering and here we were speaking about helping others. This was a man whose aim in life was to deny his own will, his very self, and we were talking about making our choices in life according to what we liked. Never perhaps had such simple replies concealed such great spiritual audacity.

His diagnosis made, he proceeded very calmly and gently to a cure. He invited us to go and pray with him: 'To teach us prayer,' as he put it. It was then that I made the greatest error of my life. I still reproach myself for it. Perhaps I was not worthy of such a blessing. Five minutes with that champion of prayer and perhaps many things in my inner world might have changed. I still do not know how to pray. Who knows if I am paying the price for that mistake? What we were afraid of, I do not know. Perhaps we were frightened that he might make us become monks. We told him that it was late and that they would be waiting for us at the Danielaioi Brotherhood, and so we asked for his blessing before leaving. We made do with asking him to pray for us. He had done us the honour of suggesting that he pray with us—or rather that we pray with him—and we just asked him to pray for us, without of course really meaning it. If we had meant it, we would have stayed. It wasn't as if we had any idea about what prayer was in any case.

So we took his blessing and left for the Danielaioi, happy that we had avoided danger.

'May all be well and may God enlighten you always,' he said wishing us goodbye in a fatherly manner.

I may have left in body, yet in my mind and my heart I stayed behind. The landscape, the people and the scenes I had witnessed remained deeply impressed on my being.

About twenty years later, God counted me worthy to offer communion from my unworthy hands to Fr Ephraim—that giant of obedience, that champion of the prayer of the heart, perhaps the last hesychast of our era—when he fell ill and had to spend two weeks in Athens. The atmosphere in the room was one of mystical compunction. In his clear eyes and in the holiness of his life you saw reflected the mystery of the deified man and the majesty of the soul united to Christ. His repentance welled up from the spring of the grace of God and as his tears flowed they mixed with the blood of Christ.

Fr Ephraim spoke more with his eyes than with words. He wrote more books with his tears than he had ever read with his eyes. The sighs of his prayer filled the 'libraries' of the lives of so many people. His presence sustained Athos, the Church, indeed the whole world, in our sterile and barren times.

He was someone who always inspired me. I was fortunate enough to serve the Liturgy in the small chapel at his cell, one morning in 1976. All that somehow wiped out the foolishness of my former denial. I too prayed with him. In his cell, three years before he fell asleep in the Lord, he placed his hands around my unwise head and together with his blessings—as he was wont to do—he offered me his prayer out loud.

Chapter 9

SKETES - THE FRAGRANCE OF HOLY RELICS - THE RETURN TO THE WORLD

Tuesday, 18 August 1971 at the Danielaioi Brotherhood. A meal with fresh bream caught by Fr Stephen. He walked up and down the steep path to the jetty with the same ease that we would go from room to room. We set off for the skete of Little St Anne in the afternoon. Our first visit was to the Thomades Brotherhood. There were three of them, all silversmiths. They made a fine community. The elder had the wisdom of another age. He was a man of little education and knowledge, yet he had great insight and understanding. They offered us something to eat, explained their craft to us, and we left rather hurriedly to go and find Fr Gerasimos of Little St Anne.

He was as noble, polite and gracious as he had seemed to us at Ouranoupolis. I will never forget his old-fashioned way of speaking. I could have listened to him for hours. Fortunately, he was not a shy speaker. There was a wonderfully friendly atmosphere: it was as if we had known each other for years. The walls of his small, simple cell were covered in bookshelves. It was here that this man spent endless hours at work, diving into the past to meet the saints, fathoming their lives in order to discover their hidden depths and, through the grace of God, writing hymns and services in their honour.

Before we left, we venerated the cave of Saints Dionysius and Mitrophan, and then the relics of St Nektarios of Aegina and St George of Ioannina, which exuded such a strong aroma that I voiced my amazement and perplexity. I genuinely couldn't understand how this could happen.

A few years later I visited the Monastery of Grigoriou with a friend of mine. In the evening, I asked the Abbot about this phenomenon. Acting very naturally, he brought out a small relic of St Gregory Palamas for us to venerate. After we had all kissed it he asked us if it had smelt fragrant to us.

'Perhaps…maybe…I don't know,' I said.

'No,' he replied, 'it has no perfume. But if we were to say the Canon to the saint, the whole place would be filled with an inexpressible fragrance. Do you want us to try and see?'

'We don't need to perform experiments on the saints,' my friend said.

'Yes, we do,' I said to myself stubbornly.

We lost the opportunity. The strange piety of my fellow pilgrim was respected. But God did not leave my desire unfulfilled for long.

The fragrance given out by holy relics is one of the most remarkable manifestations of the presence and grace of God. To become aware of it is an overpowering experience. The saint is so alive that this spiritual vitality manifests itself as a 'spiritual fragrance' permeating the soul, transfiguring the body and flowing out from the relic. The aroma is a confirmation of their sanctity and eternal life and we experience it with our senses as something unutterably beautiful. It has often been the case that I have venerated the relics of a saint without noticing anything in particular, only then to chant the service or hymn to the saint and for the whole place to fill with a wonderful fragrance. Or someone might approach a relic with prayer borne of suffering, in humble faith or deep devotion and the saint reveals the grace of God in the form of a sweet fragrance.

We left the Skete of Little St Anne at about 5 o'clock in the afternoon and started out for the Skete of St Anne. After a few minutes we passed by the Hermitage of the Resurrection where the elder Savvas lived. The view was magnificent. You could look at it for hours. It was something I could never get used to—I have always found leaving that place very difficult. It is impossible to describe what the eyes behold and the heart feels. Here earthly and heavenly beauty are woven together in a unique and masterly way. Here 'the invisible things of Him since the creation of the world are clearly seen, being perceived through the things that are made, even his everlasting power and divinity.'[37]

I spent the next night at the hut of Fr Anthimos. Late that evening, once he had finished hearing confessions, he asked a young man who was waiting with me if he was married.

'Yes,' he replied, 'I have three children.'

He looked crushed and disappointed at this answer. He had not been expecting it—he had wanted to hear something else. Whatever the case, he assured him that he could still be saved. As for me, unfortunately, the possibility was still there. I was still unmarried. With great affection he pointed to the lights of the village Sarti on the peninsula of Sithonia opposite.

'There, is hell,' he said, 'here, is paradise.'

It seemed that I chose to prefer hell. I was drawn to the world. That's where I felt more at home.

From the Skete of St Anne, by way of New Skete, we went to the Monastery of St Paul. An imposing building, it stood at the foot of the mountain. Everything was so spotlessly clean that it

---

[37] Rom. 1:20.

gleamed. The walls of the corridors were covered in frescos and sayings from the Fathers that had been arranged in such a way that there was no escape for one's thoughts. We were led to the reception room. The guest master, a monk of about fifty, brought us the usual tray of hospitality. Sombre and taciturn, he was very tall—he must have been over six foot—and his movements were heavy and slow. A kind man, although unsmiling. He was whispering something over and over again. I observed him carefully. He was saying the prayer 'Lord, Jesus Christ, have mercy upon me.' I tried to look him in the eyes but it was impossible to meet his glance. His peacefulness was reflected not in his face—for you couldn't see it—but in his whole bearing.[38]

Another pilgrim who was there asked, 'Father, how tall are you?'

'Lord have mercy,' said Fr Mitrophan: that was the guest master's name.

There was silence for a while. After a few minutes, someone else piped up:

'How long have you been in the monastery?'

'Glory to you, O God,' was his reply.

Another period of silence followed.

---

[38] Here the word used for peacefulness is '*hesychia*'. The monk truly reflected the peacefulness of the hesychast who practices the prayer of the heart, i.e. the Jesus Prayer that he was saying.

'Father, how many monks are there in the monastery?' came the third question.

'Come, and I will show you to your rooms,' he answered, and we all stood up.

Once we had settled in, we went for a stroll in the courtyard.

There we came across a white-haired old monk of about eighty with the face, and soul, of a child. He was holding a bunch of grapes and patiently picking off the grapes one by one. He began to talk to us about the Kingdom of God, the treasure of our 'souls of diamond' and our salvation, which, however, he considered rather difficult. He was clearly concerned about his own salvation. His eyes filled with tears and he asked us to pray for him. Someone asked if they could take his photograph.

'What do you need a photograph for?' he objected.

'To remember you,' the pilgrim insisted.

'You should keep heaven and hell as your constant remembrance,' replied the monk, destroying for good every hope of imprinting on paper his blessed countenance, the face of a child of some eighty years old.

In the evening, after Compline, the Abbot, Fr Andreas, invited us to come and see him. We sat talking in the darkness for nearly two hours, with only a paraffin lamp for light. With the rugged features of a Cephalonian islander, hollowed out by a life of austerity and asceticism, he made a heroic figure. In his dry and somewhat hoarse voice he spoke to us frankly about current Church matters and the 'dangers' of ecumenism, and lastly the need for frequent Holy Communion. I warmed to the scene, his manly fortitude and his candour.

What I cannot forget, however, is the night office. I could not say that the *katholikon,* the main church of the monastery, inspired me. I was put off by the cold marble iconostasis and icons in the western style. But the calm peacefulness of the priest who was serving, the pious readiness and briskness of the monks and the sound of an old monk who was chanting in a voice full of contrition all created a sense of great sorrow just at the thought that all this would soon be over. I had never experienced something so devoutly peaceful and serene. Even today, what remains in my memory is the feeling of a perfect harmony of rhythm, light, intensity, naturalness and sweetness: a unique combination of external factors that enabled the turbulent world of the soul to quieten down—that internal world so troubled by the endless distractions of our senses. It was a rare reflection of heavenly peace that these people so naturally and unsuspectingly lived, people who had chosen to live in complete surrender to the will of God humbly, simply and free from care.

The last night of our pilgrimage was spent at the Monastery of Grigoriou—a very clean, and very strict monastery. It was a wonderful day and we sat on our balconies looking out at the magnificent sunset. Everyone was sitting outside on their balconies. The monks were in their cells. What were they doing? I thought what they were missing out on. How could they? What was it they enjoyed instead?

As all these thoughts crowded in on my mind I felt my spontaneous response to the natural world taking second place to the deeper spiritual need for the truth.

It was the day of our departure from Mount Athos. We set off from Daphne at 2 o'clock in the afternoon, on 21 August by the Old Calendar. After a two-hour journey we arrived at Ouranoupolis, on 3 September by the New. Another world awaited us. Here they used another calendar. We had moved ahead thirteen days in time, but spiritually we were centuries behind. Here Byzantine time meant nothing.[39] Here was variety, colour, noise and tourists; here were restaurants, popular Greek songs, all kinds of dress, families, women with small children, bicycles and motorbikes; but no Athos. Here

---

[39] According to Byzantine time the day begins at sunset. Depending on the time of year, clocks on Mount Athos are three to six hours ahead of local Greek time.

was earth, but no heaven. Arriving by boat at Ouranoupolis was indeed like arriving back on earth with a bump.

PART TWO
THE INVISIBLE ATHOS

Chapter 1

THE LIFE AND DORMITION
OF THE 'IMMORTAL ONES'

When I left the Holy Mountain, although I at once felt at home, I was filled with a profound sense of nostalgia. I missed the daringness of the buildings, the aridity of the desert, the daily pattern of life in the monasteries and the sense of another world full of hope, depth and substance. But what I missed principally were the vibrant figures of the monks, the hidden heritage of that holy place.

We disembarked and straightaway ran to catch the bus to Thessalonica. Our haste was the first indication that we were back in this new world that was yet so familiar. After a short while two women got on. They started arguing about whose seat was whose: shrill tones and shrill tempers. Some other people also began shouting in an effort to pacify them. The radio was playing some songs that made me feel nauseous. The cigarette smoke was unbearable. Someone started complaining about why we were late in setting off. Two swear-words cut through the air.

I wondered what all this had to do with the

'Glory to you, O God' of the monk who had been watering his garden in Karyes; the 'Lord have Mercy' of Fr Mitrophan and the deep sighs of Fr Paisios. My own sighs of regret at how I could readjust so suddenly to the earthly 'heaven' of the town of Ouranoupolis after the paradise of Mount Athos seemed to confirm the division within me between what inspired me and what in the end I chose. This divorce inside me bore out my attachment to this world.

But what was my relation to that other, strange world that I had just got to know and that seemed so real to me? What was my relation to that world in which the closest ties are those between joy and sorrow, poverty and riches, life and death, God and man?

I remembered how at the Monastery of St Paul, as I had been walking up the stairs of the guest house, I had noticed a saying on the wall: 'If you die before you die, then you won't die when you die.' The monks of Mount Athos live immortality more intensely than everyday life. They walk amongst you 'always carrying in the body the death of Jesus'.[40] You see them after they have died and their bodies give out the fragrance of imperishability and eternal life.

---

[40] 2 Cor. 4: 10.

Fr Mitrophan was such an unknown, anonymous and unrecognized monk, whom I had the blessing to meet later when I spent about twenty months at the monastery of St Paul. I did not meet him exactly. You cannot 'get to know' people like him. These secret treasures of the Holy Mountain usually leave this world an unfathomed mystery. We simply get to know *about* them.

They knew very little of his past life. And of course we could discover even less about his present inner life. He had been married and had come to the monastery in 1964 when he was approaching fifty, just after he had lost his wife. After twenty five years he still wore the same shoes he had had when he first became a monk, the same habit and cassock: shoes mended a thousand and one times, a habit covered in umpteen square patches of all sorts of dark hues that were variously faded, and a monastic *koukouli*[41] buffed by use. Thrown over his huge but light body, all was immaculately clean, enfolding this kindly and serenely peaceful figure and embracing his supremely gentle and noble appearance. These veteran but spotless and cherished patches were the best covering for the seamless garment[42] of his monastic integrity: the fact that

---

[41] A monastic veil worn on top of the monastic hat.

[42] John 19: 23.

his cost of living was almost zero underlined how completely he had renounced the world and his total estrangement from earthly consolations and anything ephemeral and corruptible.

During the thirty years or so he had spent in the monastery he might have uttered no more than thirty words of worldly conversation. A few years ago they had found him in his cell sitting on a chair, his head resting on cushions, and with the prayer-rope warm in his hands, his last breath breathed, leaving us with the sublime remembrance of a cenobitic hesychast.[43] He slipped into eternity with unique ease and passed through the door completely unobserved.

I encountered other 'men of violence'[44] at the Monastery of St Paul. Fr George was one such monk of rare virtue. His cell was right next to mine.

---

[43] A cenobium is a monastery where all the monks eat together in the same refectory rather than leading independent lives (see note 29). Here a 'cenobitic hesychast' is to be distinguished from a hesychast who is a hermit.

[44] The word used here in Greek is '*viastis*' or 'man of violence', which literally means 'the one who exercises "violence" on himself'. It is the word used by monks of those ascetics who live an especially austere and strict life. St John Climacus writes: '[to be a] monk means to constantly do violence to one's nature' (Homily 1 on Renunciation, para. 10), and the Lord Himself said, 'the Kingdom of Heaven suffers violence, and the violent take it by force' (Matt. 11: 12).

The ascetic effort of his last years consisted in the uncompromising struggle for unceasing prayer, insistence on standing up through the long services despite his age and unbearable back pain, not washing at all and putting up with dirtiness and untidiness. His cell exuded neglect in about the same way as his body did. You could tell even if you had a cold. For company he had a few icons, his threadbare prayer-rope, and unsurprisingly a wide variety of creepy crawlies and other animals that found refuge, as well as a fair amount of food, in his cell. It was not on a few occasions that I too had visitors from his entourage. From time to time ticks from Fr George's 'cage' would leave their mark on my pampered frame. It seemed to me an unbearable discomfort. He never uttered a word. Perhaps they had devoured his body, and were parading up and down on the remains of his toughened bones. I was full of admiration at his steadfastness, fortitude and endurance.

I remember how in 1988 they sent us, together with a novice, as representatives to the Great Lavra for the feast-day of St Athanasios the Athonite. At about 5 o'clock in the afternoon the jeep stood waiting for us at the monastery gate, ready to take us down to the harbour from where we were to take the boat. Fr George, who was then eighty, had already descended on foot. We, the younger ones, went down by car. On the boat I caught sight of him in a corner, his head bowed, literally hanging off his prayer-rope. He did not speak to us, for he clearly did not wish to destroy his treasured quietude.

When we arrived at the harbour of the Lavra a van was waiting to take us up to the monastery, a walk of about forty minutes, uphill all the way. Fr George had disappeared. He must have gone off to pray somewhere, I thought. But when we had got half way, we saw him walking up. The driver stopped to pick him up. But Fr George gestured to him to drive on. I could not understand what was going on. Afterwards they told me that, in 1963, as a representative of the Monastery of St Paul, he had reacted very strongly to the opening of the first road on Mount Athos, from Daphne to Karyes, which had been built in order to make it easier for the officials who had come for the millennium celebrations to get about. True to his original position, he never got into a car on Mount Athos.

Even when we arrived at the monastery not only did he refuse to rest before the all-night vigil service, but he did not even want to leave his bag in the room allocated to us.

'We haven't come here to rest, or to sleep, or to be shown honour. We have come to labour, to spend the night in prayer and to be humbled. Only in this way can we move the saint to hear our entreaties,' he said.

He went straight to church. It was about 7 o'clock in the evening. The vigil started at 9 o'clock on the eve of the feast, and finished, together with the meal, at 12:30 the next afternoon. Fr George did not leave the church at all. He stayed awake, struggling and praying, and standing for more than seventeen hours.

The boat was to leave at 5 o'clock in the afternoon to take us back to our monastery. I lay down for three hours in a quiet room. I relaxed bodily, but my mind and my conscience did not rest for a minute. The constant thought of Fr George did not let me. The car that belonged to the Lavra arrived to take us down to the harbour. About fifty metres away we could see Fr George alone and praying with his prayer-rope, which he continued to do on the boat.

We reached the harbour of St Paul at about 6 o'clock in the evening. My heroic neighbour walked past me. His eyes were all red; his soul pure white, and his life full of spiritual fruits. He passed the jeep that was waiting for us and carried on walking up the hill to the monastery, the mount of his constancy, the mount of his sanctification. I felt ashamed of my littleness of heart. I wanted to imitate him, but I was unable to. He was eighty. I was less than half his age. He was twice as old as me, but much more advanced in terms of spiritual vigour and infinitely richer in divine grace. God granted him rest from his earthly labours in 1998. He fulfilled his heavenly desires forever.

Such were the pearls concealed in the treasure house of the Monastery of St Paul. Such riches are the priceless spiritual heritage in the crypt of the Holy Mountain.

On Mount Athos I also came to know the living presence of monks after death. I witnessed the 'signs' of God's grace in their lives, at the moment when science and human sense and understanding assert the irreversibility of their end. As soon as the weightiness of this life falls away, then the fullness and vitality of their immortal and eternal presence comes to life.

It was in a cell in the depths of the Athonite desert that I, now as a priest-monk, had a wonderful experience of the dormition of an ascetic who was known to God, but unknown to me and to most of the world. I remember, years ago, when I was visiting two friends of mine who were monks at a hermitage in Kafsokalyvia,[45] how an elder, who lived nearby, informed us that he had a very important announcement to make. The news was that he sensed that he was about to leave this world. As

---

[45] A skete at the southern tip of the peninsula of the Holy Mountain.

they say in the monasteries, he asked us to work our prayer-ropes all together in order to ease the departure of his soul. Such were his yearning and thirst to leave this world that they were beyond us, but we heeded his resolve and began to pray: 'Lord, Jesus Christ, grant rest to the soul of your servant, the monk X.' He started to make the sign of the cross and to repeat: 'Christ is Risen.' He made the sign of the cross again, once more saying 'Christ is Risen.' We continued our prayer: 'Lord, Jesus Christ, grant rest to the soul of your servant.'

As time went by his voice gradually became more peaceful, and all the time more weak: what he was gaining in heavenly expression, he was losing in terms of earthly time. After a few minutes he gathered together all his strength and, in a voice full of praise, said, 'Christ is Risen! He is Risen indeed!' tilted his head and breathed out a half breath: that half of the whole breath that God had given him, as he has given to all of us; the half that is necessary for the body to stay alive. And he kept the other half: the half that is essential for the soul to have eternal life; the breath that is the most valuable possession of every person in this life; the breath that works as fuel for the next life. The room immediately filled with a heavenly fragrance. I do not know if this was due to the breath that he breathed out or the one that he retained. The first was the affirmation of a holy life; the second the promise of an eternal future. In some miraculous manner his body maintained its flexibility and warmth and exuded the scent of his sanctity as a form of consolation. Our eyes filled with tears. We were not lamenting the one who had departed: we felt sorrow for those who remained.

An abbot of one of the monasteries narrated a similar story. He was very moved as he spoke. In his monastery there was a monk who was fairly remiss. He rarely went to services. He would go into church, venerate the icons and then disappear. It was as if he could not remain in one place for long. Nobody knew where he went. Nobody knew what he did. And he had another failing. He drank. His breath always smelt of wine. He did not bother anyone. He never spoke ill of anyone. But his life was not the life of a monk.

The years passed and he died. The brotherhood was plunged into agony: anguish for his soul and for his salvation. He had left unprepared: he had not taken communion for years, at least as far as they could tell. They spent the night sighing in heartfelt prayer, their eyes filled with tears.

The moment of the burial arrived. The monks surrounding his dead body were not lamenting the fact that they had lost him as much as suffering because of his spiritual condition at his death. But at the moment when they lowered him into the tomb, instead of taking a last look at the monk, they all glanced at each other in wonder. The most simple-hearted of the brothers broke the awkward silence:

'Elder, his body is giving out a fragrance,' he said, expressing what everyone was thinking and no one dared to admit.

And indeed, the air was filled with a wonderful fragrance. For days afterwards his grave bore witness to some hidden magnificence and affirmed the mystery of God. He who had smelt of wine in this life gave out the aroma of divine grace and commendation. Beyond outward appearances and behind his weaknesses there lay concealed the treasure of a saintly life and a monastic soul who now prays for his fellow monks, and in whom the Spirit of God forever dwells.

How different is God to man! How different is His judgment from ours! The Holy Mountain: its name contains two words. The word 'mountain'—something you can climb with your feet, and the word 'holy'—which you may 'ascend' through your prayer. On the mountain you discover peaks. On the inner ascent caves are revealed to you. The caves of the mountain conceal much more than its summit reveals: for the caverns are hidden, while the peaks can be seen.

Chapter 2

THE DESERT
OF MOUNT ATHOS

I have always been fascinated by the region of the Athonite desert, that is, the whole mountain range from the Great Lavra to the Monastery of St Paul, the refuge of ascetics and hesychasts. I was enchanted by its splendour. Here my imagination could easily give shape and form to my unceasing desire for the extreme, for that which lies beyond our reason, the heroic, the heavenly and the divine. Its prospect produced in me an inexpressible sense of awe and the recollection of it filled my soul with consolation and hope.

This place is a very singular type of desert. The scenery is austere: dry rocks, dwarf bushes, scattered trees and dry earth. There are hardly any sounds: now and again a bird sings or, more often, a bird of prey wings by, reminding you of the presence of life. The rustle of the wind in the bushes or the whistling of the mountain air caresses your ears. As you listen you are startled by a lizard slithering by or a rock falling unexpectedly. The scents are delicate but distinctive. Apart from the wild flowers you can detect the subtle smells of stone, earth, the fresh air and the sea breeze. All the senses work at their lowest intensity. You are constrained to use them unlike anywhere else.

The greatest surprise of all is the encounter with an ascetic. Here there are very few of them. The ones that do live here keep themselves hidden. Shut away in their hermitages, they gives themselves over to 'the keeping of the mind', and 'in their hearts are the highways to zion'[46] and while praying they climb 'the narrow and hard way'.[47] If they are obliged to leave the 'arena' of their hut or their cave, their earthly bodies are so dry and thin that even if you do come across them, they blend into the landscape and you can't see them: you do not even notice them and they pass by unobserved.

As your senses settle down and the possibility of meeting another person becomes practically non-existent, you discover 'new' sights, sounds and smells—ones of a different order. You cross the desert in the middle of winter and waves of spring smells wash over you without your being able to explain where they come from. The place has become holy. Everything has been kneaded

---

[46] Psalms 84: 5.
[47] A reference to Matt. 7: 14.

together with miracles, and radiates transcendence. The presence of the saints is made apparent in many different ways. God reveals His grace and makes you certain of His presence in a very subtle manner. Future reality seems to have broken into the present. Earthen man becomes nothing and gains everything. He is laid bare and is 'clad in white garments'.[48] He hungers and yet is satiated. He lacks for everything, struggles, lives ascetically and experiences the fullness of the promises of the beatitudes.[49] He lives the death and resurrection of his senses, their transfiguration from the physical to the spiritual. He prepares to recognize God and, if his heart is pure, the possibility of a divine encounter becomes a reality.

Just as in a desert the reflection makes things in the distance seem very near and the haziness gives way to clearness and limpidity, so in the desert of Mount Athos you can hear and see distant sounds and visions. Beyond the human and corruptible you can discern the holy and incorruptible. Here someone can see God clearly and realize that His presence is near.

Here you can hear the hum of unceasing prayer and fallen man in his constant sighing. Here the fate

---

[48] Rev. 3: 5.
[49] Matt. 5: 3-11.

of the world is held in the balance. Here God strains His ears and here He decides. For this is the place of His rest. In this desert one can hear the echo of angelic hymns, the praise-filled silence of the saints, and the melody of the eternal divine word.

In the desert of the Holy Mountain it is easier to meet an angel than a man. The landscape is so harsh that man cannot endure it and so immaterial that angels long to be here. Here they are in abundance. The environment is more hospitable to them. It reminds one more of heaven than of earth. Here it is easier for a man to recognize an angel than for an angel to recognize a man. For here man, the hermits, have eyes that can see angels, whereas the angels cannot conceive that such men could exist. Those who can bear it here can see but they cannot be seen: they are more like angels than human beings; they are more heavenly than earthly; they are eternal rather than temporal; they are more divine than human. In them God finds rest and the angels are amazed. 'The angelic ranks were amazed by your life in the flesh', so says the hymn in honour of the father of Athonite monks, St Athanasios of Mount Athos. One experiences intensely this wonder of the angels simply by beholding the environment and breathing the air.

Such is the purity of the desert that it enters into you. Without realizing it your soul becomes transparent. Without making any effort your inner world is revealed. You confess spontaneously. And if you are blessed enough to meet a hermit he is able to see into your soul without difficulty. Here people have eyes and souls that can be seen.

Ever since I was a child I had felt disappointed with the nature of man. But I was inspired by his image as potentiality: what man could do or become. Our potential to become heavenly enthralled me more than the angelic world. I was moved more by seeing the divine in a person rather than imagining it in God. The godlikeness of man is perhaps the only thing that impressed me more than the godliness of God… What surpasses His godliness is the mystery of the divine Incarnation. God's self-emptying or *kenosis* is a greater mystery than the deification or *theosis* of man!

The nature of angels and God is compatible with their essence. Only God in the person of Christ 'assumed what he was not, retaining at the same time his divinity'.[50] But man, whose fallen nature is marked by perversion and misery, when he lives with an eternal perspective he acquires god-like habits and a heavenly countenance: when he sheds the outer skin of his nature, when he becomes what he is not, without denying what he is, then that man

---

[50] Hymns of the Praises from the Matins for Christmas Day.

startles us as a miracle, moves us as a consolation, and becomes a vision of what we can become.

The sudden protuberance that is Athos reminds me of a swollen belly that has borne and continues to give birth to such men for more than a thousand years, people who 'escaped whatever is contrary to nature and preserved what is according to nature' and above all 'became worthy of gifts transcending their nature'.[51]

Here the divine element in human nature is preserved. Here the dignity and nobility of what it is to be human is retained. Here the return to Paradise takes place; here we see 'the reformation to the ancient beauty',[52] 'the reinstatement to the old created beauty' and 'the resurrection of the image, as it was before the fall, is fulfilled'.[53] Returning to the state of paradise is more earth-shattering than being there. It is more divine: not as a movement, because it reminds one of the Fall—God does not return—but as something magnificent, as a miracle. Here the hope of becoming 'after his likeness' becomes a reality. His grace is constantly being confirmed. Doubts about his existence disintegrate. His presence is constantly revealed.

---

[51] St Nikodimos of Mount Athos, *Doxastikon* hymn of Matins for the feast-day of the saints of Mount Athos.

[52] *Evlogitaria* hymns from the funeral service.

[53] *Apolytikio* hymn for Christmas Eve.

The sight of Athos inspired me much more than listening to a Beethoven symphony or the conception of Newton's genius. It moved me more than the most original or impressive scientific achievement or idea. The aesthetic attraction of art, and the splendour and charm of intellectual greatness seem like shadows compared to the subtle beauty and humble magnificence of experiencing the presence of the Holy Spirit.

Athos, this hidden, secret miracle, this protrusion, this magnificent rock not only brings forth mystically what is new: it gives birth to the superhuman, to godlikeness in human beings. Here man acquires godliness.

Chapter 3

GOD HAS CHOSEN
THE FOOLISH THINGS
OF THE WORLD

Mount Athos is the mountain of the quietude of God, the mountain of divine ascent, yet its highest peak is humility. Its every nook, every characteristic and every detail of its rule and its way of life, conceals the greatness of genuine humility that is exalted.[54]

There are humble people who, quite by themselves and out of spiritual prudence, have chosen the way of obscurity and insignificance. Their harvest is a secret one of the heart. They are gifted people who do not waste the gifts of God. They are people of virtue, ability, knowledge and experience, but they bury themselves without expecting any reward in this world or in the next. Blessed souls! The scourge of vainglory has not touched them. The world ignores them and looks upon them differently. It is continually unjust towards them and misun-

---

[54] Matt 23: 12.

derstands them. And they calmly walk 'the way of the Lord'.

Apart from these there is another category of people. There are those whom God conceals in order that He might hide Himself within them: marginal characters, who are naïve, and have obvious faults, who are psychologically unstable, who in some cases are repugnant, 'fools of the world', and who cause people to avoid them. And yet those very people whom the world disdains God chooses as His dwelling and transforms into instruments of His grace.

In our monastery there lived a monk called Fr Charalambos, who was disregarded by all. If he drummed up the courage to say something, you could barely understand him. A certain bodily disability made it incredibly difficult for him to walk. He could only just about pull himself along. When he had left his home on the island of Lemnos he took the boat and appeared at the monastery with a donkey and a quilt. That was all he owned. His relatives and siblings had duped him out of his inheritance. He was not very old and he looked like someone on whom you could easily impose your will, and if you were a little impudent you could make fun of him.

His eyes were always full of tears and red from crying. It was very difficult to meet his gaze. A threadbare prayer-rope twisted constantly in his hand. If you were spiritually perceptive you realized that underneath there was something unusual about this person. He was kind and gentle in his manner, and reserved and unassuming in his speech. He spoke more with his whole being and presence than his lips. And he revealed a great deal.

One of the younger brothers liked to play jokes on him. He wanted Fr Charalambos to remind him about something three times a day. He made him wake him up at a late hour every evening, supposedly so that he might begin his rule of prayer. Fr Charalambos would literally drag himself to this monk's cell in order to help him.

'Why do you trouble him so?' I asked the scurrilous monk.

'Don't you worry about him. He is a bit simple; he hasn't got anything else to do. That's how he fills his time,' he answered.

'Dear brother, have you ever suspected that this man whom you torment might conceal such glory, such that you can't even imagine?'

'Well, if you are right, then let's not tire out our old lazy-bones again,' he said to me sarcastically, and left.

A few days later I was passing by Fr Charalambos's cell. His door was slightly ajar and I knocked softly. I called out who I was and he asked me to come in. It was the first time I had entered his cell. I had never seen such a bare interior. On the wall there was only one icon of the Lord—nothing else at all. There was a wooden table and no chair, only a little stool. No books. Instead of bed there was a wooden bench. No blankets. No cupboard either. On the windowsill there was a glass. If I remember rightly there was not anything else. In this inhospitable and empty space he spent hours on end, without any form of consolation.

'Fr Charalambos, how do you spend your time here?' I asked.

'I say my rule of prayer, I practice obedience to the abbot and I await my departing.'

'But don't you feel the need for any form of companionship?'

'Where can I find better companions than in our Lord, the Mother of God and the saints? Fr Pachomios used to come and see me, but he has been punishing me for the last few days now by not coming.'

'Why did Fr Pachomios come here?'

'He wanted me to remind him about some things he had to do and to wake him up so he could say his prayers.'

'But from what I can see, you don't have a clock. There isn't anything in the room. How do you know what time it is?'

'I don't know what time it is. I don't need to either. After saying Small Compline and the prayer to my guardian angel, I ask him to let me know when it is time to go. If it is night, he wakes me up. If it is the day, he opens the door and reminds me."

'Do you know your guardian angel?'

'Of course I do. He is my constant companion. At night, when I have difficulty going up the stairs, I ask him to wake the other monks. When we have a vigil service and I feel sleepy I pray and say to him: "Holy angel, you know how many people suffer from insomnia, how many toss and turn in their beds trying to get to sleep. Take my drowsiness and use it to seal their eyes." That is what Fr Paisios told me to say, and that is what I do.'

This was how he overcame the problem of how to stay awake and keep his vigil. Surely many people, as a result of his prayers, would have overcome the problem of how to get to sleep. Our alliance and cooperation with our guardian angel is a great thing.

In general, the relation of the saints with the spiritual world and the grace of God is something very subtle. Habit, inner self-sufficiency, the sense that one has knowledge and understanding, audacity and familiarity create the false sense of the divine mystery and weaken one's ability to recognize it. In contrast, modesty, meek unassertiveness and artlessness are expressions of the innocent purity of the soul and demonstrate a humility that transforms man into a 'chosen vessel' and that attracts the grace of God. The mystery of God cannot be looked for, but when it is given and revealed, then it should be humbly accepted. Our relation with everything holy must be governed by the humble sense of the uniqueness of that first experience, and not by the ease of repeated habit.

Fr Haralambos remained unrecognized even by the monks in his own monastery. Blessed is he who stood humbly close to him and in putting aside his own self was instructed by the majesty of his invisibility. Life next to a saint who does not realize the gift he has but who is covered by the grace of God, who lives discounted by others but established in the memory of God, is despised by his brothers but converses with the holy angels, is unjustly treated and ridiculed by others but himself prays for the whole world, whom everyone thinks is unimportant but for God is important, who has no knowledge of theology but lives it as revelation, is itself a revelation. To humble yourself before your brothers is a more certain path than to have contrition before God. The indirect grace you 'borrow' from a humble person speaks more than the grace that you receive directly from God. To rejoice in someone else's gift is greater than to enjoy your own, even if it has been given to you by God.

Chapter 4

THE MEETING WITH GOD THROUGH TRANSCENDENTAL RISKS

Once, when I went to see him, Fr Paisios spoke to me about the 'other' kind of logic. He told me how the most rational people are those who deny, and essentially transcend their reason, the so-called fools for Christ. A certain Fr Euthymios, who lived in Vigla, had, through the grace of God, persuaded everyone that he was mad. He recommended that I should go to see him, but with caution lest I be scandalized.

I left for the Monastery of Iviron, where I spent the night. The next day I took the boat for the Great Lavra. Onboard were about twenty five to thirty people at most, the majority of whom were laymen. How wonderful that there were so few monks, I thought. They do not travel in this world, nor around Athos without good reason. They journey elsewhere...

Some people had a slight misunderstanding and a terrific quarrel erupted. How out of place it seemed in the world of Athos. Some others tried to intervene, calling upon the sanctity of the place. The tension grew. A charming and simple monk took the initiative. With a remarkable display of humour he diffused the situation, demonstrating that everything was much simpler than we all thought, and the threats were transformed into laughter. And this too seemed to jar with the Athos of contrition and tears.

My gaze alighted on two monks. My eyes and imagination began to work more than my ears. Instead of listening to the jokes I felt the need to fathom something profound and unknown. One of them was in his early forties, and the other about forty-five, his beard just beginning to turn white. It was as if they were unaware of anything going on around them. The sweetness of their faces was extraordinary. They were not troubled either by the argument or by the laughter—they were completely oblivious. They seemed to accept everything tranquilly, without becoming part of it. The peacefulness of their faces surpassed 'every understanding'.[55] I was entranced by their free but steady gaze. Their bodily stillness and the intentness of their bearing betrayed an inner strength, quietude and profundity. I was overawed by the naturalness of

---

[55] Phil. 4:7.

their spiritual condition. They were completely at a remove from the boat and its load and yet their faces had such a good-natured and kind expression. Their hands swiftly and steadily embraced the knots of their prayer-ropes one after the other, revealing their concentration of thought, the watchfulness of their spiritual intellect and their constant awareness of standing before God. Their minds and hearts were at work elsewhere.

They were turned towards the sea and I to the mountain. They were waiting for the grace and mercy of God to enter their hearts: I was looking for new things to satisfy the curiosity of my mind. I caught sight of a Russian onion dome high up on the mountain in between the chestnut trees. The person sitting next to me was making the sign of the cross and I asked him what it was. He told me that it was the cell of St Artemios in Provata where Fr Ephraim and his disciples lived. They were twenty three in all and they practiced the prayer of the heart. They did not laugh or talk. They followed the rule of silence and prayer. Their ears and their eyes were attuned to the other world, a world I both ignored and refused to draw near to. I was filled with envy at the magnificence of these people. I felt ashamed of my littleness of heart and sorrow at my spiritual emptiness. Inasmuch as these monks were strangers to me, so too was I a foreigner to their spirit and their way of life.

The boat arrived at its destination and I spent the night at the Great Lavra. I was headed for Fr Euthymios's in Vigla. All that night I could not stop thinking about what the next day would bring. After the Divine Liturgy the next morning I enquired as to where exactly he lived. They told me that he was the monk who had taken communion—the only person to have done so. How disappointing! I had not noticed him and the opportunity was gone. They told me that he was not right in the head, and having received this confirmation I set off. I walked for over an hour. It was terribly hot. The vegetation was very scanty and sparse: a disconsolate landscape. In the distance could be discerned the Romanian skete of St John the Baptist. A relatively short way away and scattered all around were low huts, sunken in hollows in the ground. A real desert.

I decided to approach the nearest hut. No sound came from it. Someone lived there, however. A vest and a tattered habit were hanging on a washing line. They must belong to Fr Euthymios, I thought. There was a sense of general untidiness. I approached very hesitantly and cautiously. I must not startle him, for if I did he might startle me. That is what Fr Paisios had told me. Suddenly, amongst the rusty cans, broken chairs and pots and pans strewn about, I spied a head covered by a straw hat. The man was not wearing a habit. Instead he wore a pair of jeans and braces, but no vest. He looked at me steadily and blankly, fixing his eyes on me. I was gripped by fear. I could not think or feel anything. I was overcome by awkwardness. My legs floundered under me and my tongue was all in knots. I faltered and mumbled, 'Your blessing'. Without answering he asked in a severe tone, 'What do you want?'

'It's Fr Euthymios I'm looking for,' I answered.

'You won't find any such person here,' he answered so adamantly that he only confirmed his identity.

Beginning to regain my self-possession, I tried to make him say something but it was impossible. He completely ignored me. He would not open his mouth, and I could not think of anything else to say. I waited to see if he would offer me anything to eat or drink, but he did not do that either. I got up to go and he seemed especially relieved.

I wanted to see him and he was struggling to hide from me. What contrary paths we were following! He, of course, achieved what he wanted. But as for me, what did I manage to achieve? As the feeling of the 'wildness' of our meeting receded what gradually emerged was a profound sense of reverence and sincere admiration for what I had seen, and revulsion at what I was.

I walked on for about fifteen minutes and

arrived at a point above the cave of St Athanasios. A wooden cross on the top of the rock marked the descent. Here the gradient was 90 degrees—it was completely vertical. I started going down the steps of the ladder, of which there must have been about two hundred. After a little while I reached the cave. It was the natural landscape more than the thought of the saint that inspired me to contrition. It was his heroism more than his sanctity that amazed me. I sat down for a little while. My mind stopped and my heart took over. Without noticing, I had begun to pray. The torrent of my thoughts had become breathing prayer. Here you could not think. You lived without being aware of it. I praised God from the depths of my being. My other self had emerged: perhaps it was there that I felt the desire for my calling for the first time. I made that visit in 1983. Truly, what a great help one's natural surroundings can be!

Later, in 1988, and on the instructions of Fr Paisios, I had also gone to visit two Romanian hermits in Kapsala, with a friend of mine who was a monk. We brought tomatoes, peaches, pears, a little pasta and biscuits as a present or 'blessing'. That's what we had found to buy in Karyes.

Our first encounter was with the old monk Xenophon. As soon as he heard our footsteps, and before we even got there, he shouted out joyfully,

'He is coming, fathers, he is coming.'

We listened with a mixture of surprise and wonder as he repeated this phrase a few times. Suddenly we caught sight of him in the bushes: a little old man of eighty-eight sitting astride a wicker chair with its back to his chest and his hands held up high to the sky. As soon as he saw us he broke into sobs. We could not understand what was going on. In his broken Greek he apologized and explained. For days now he had been praying to God to grant him rest. He thought that God had forgotten him. When he heard our steps and the rustle of the bushes as we made our way towards him, he had thought that his angel was approaching. As soon as he saw it was us and not his angel, he was disappointed—and rightly so. He did not say anything; we could just tell. On Mount Athos the angel is more eagerly awaited—even if he is coming to take your soul—than a man, even if he is bringing you chocolate digestives.

Once he had come to, and again through sobs, he began thanking us for our trouble and apologizing if he had upset or offended us. A few days later his angel came for him—Fr Xenophon went to his eternal rest. May we have his blessing.

It was already getting late and we also had to go and visit Fr Herodion, a Romanian hermit who was either a fool for Christ—or he was not a man.

Within ten minutes we had reached his 'rubbish tip'. The sun had already set. In a ruin of a building that was full of refuse we met a new hero. A man of eighty-two, he stood in the doorframe that had no door. His feet and hands were resting against one side, while he had leaned his back up against the other. He would spend hours in that position. He was not wearing a habit. A woollen vest and a tattered pair of trousers covered his sanctified body. There was litter everywhere. You could not see the floor. There was a layer of tins, plastic bags, corks, bottle tops, pips, peel, and whatever else one could imagine about thirty centimetres thick, or even more. This was the precious carpet in his mysterious little palace. It was of course also his mattress, if, that is, he slept lying down. The walls were splattered with coffee and orange juice stains, and instead of domestic animals there were all kinds of insects, flies, bugs and rodents.

'Your blessing, father,' my naive fellow-traveller said cheerfully.

'The blessing of the Lord,' he calmly replied. This heroic ascetic did not appear bothered by his 'ecological' surroundings in the least.

'We have brought you a little food to eat as a form of blessing,' my friend the monk continued without hesitating.

'Oh, good fathers, big thanks you. I thanks you.

Good fathers. Big thanks you,' he replied.

Taking the bag with the food and continuing to repeat these words with particular force and expressiveness, he started to throw the tomatoes and peaches over our heads against the walls of his hut. As I looked at the juice trickling down and ducked my head to avoid the volleys, I was completely at a loss. I was trying to understand what was the logic behind his 'thankfulness' and the meaning of this unusual form of monasticism.

After breaking the spaghetti into two and pouring out the contents of the packet, and throwing the biscuits as far as he could, shouting, 'Let the birds eat. Let the birds eat,' he began to talk about Judas's betrayal of Christ, the Cross and, in between inarticulate cries, to glorify the name of God.

It had already begun to get dark. In a while we would not be able to see the spectacle. We would miss what Fr Herodion appeared to be. But in the darkness of my own mind I had begun to have an inkling of what all this concealed: the rubbish, the nonsensical words and the totally unfathomable human reason of the man who was a fool for the love of Christ. I remembered the writings of Abba Isaac, who describes how these heroic saints live 'in external disorder while having internal order' and concludes: 'May God count us worthy of this

insanity.'[56] So was this the other 'human reason',
the 'logic' that Fr Paisios had told me about?

I looked back to catch one more glimpse of him.
His naturally ugly face had a wildness that came
from his way of life. It was shining in some
transcendental manner as a result of the grace of
God. The radiance was so great that my earthen
eyes and my 'blind' heart were compelled to see
unusual and unfamiliar visions of 'another' kind
and 'another' world. His mysterious countenance
lies deeply embedded in my memory.

I left and dived back into the 'rubbish' of myself.
He remained there stepping on the 'rubbish' of the
logic of this world. I thought of him and was filled
with admiration at his heroism and his powers of
endurance. Even now, while I can appreciate its
worth and greatness, I cannot grasp the workings of
his logic. For certain, reason is a greater aberration
than the foolishness of the fool for Christ. Perhaps,
however, the cross of reason is heavier than the
cross of Fr Herodion.

I dared project the logic, the prestige and the
refinement of my then recent experience of Harvard
and MIT onto the 'university' of rubbish and
foolishness. When I did so the rubbish began to
give out the fragrance of flowers, the insects to turn

---

[56] Abba Isaac, *Ascetic Homilies* (Athens, 1895), p. 105.

into birds, the ripped plastic bags into degrees and academic papers; and Fr Herodion began to appear much more 'intelligent' and successful than my Nobel prize-winning professors. Their logic seemed like a racing car; the logic of the fool for Christ is like a rocket. A car can go up to two-hundred miles per hour; a rocket travels at 18,000 miles an hour and above. A car moves along the ground; a rocket shoots straight upwards. With a car, if you go beyond its limits you will crash; with a rocket if you surpass its limits you launch yourself: you overcome the gravity of the earth; you escape; you free yourself. As fast as logical and rational people go, they still remain earth-bound. Fr Herodion left this world without having 'touched' the earth—without the earth having touched him…

Chapter 5

TREADING ON UNTRODDEN GROUND: THE RULE OF THE *AVATON*[57]

How wonderful is the logic of the Holy Mountain! It produces people who are profound, true, genuine, simple and human: that can be seen. It creates heavenly, eternal, God-like people who are beyond our understanding: that can be discovered. On Athos needs have been abolished and desires transformed. Its contact with anything earthly, worldly, ephemeral or human is a similar relation to comparing the size of its 'capital' Daphne with the area of the whole peninsula. The Holy Mountain takes from the world only that which it needs. As for desires, they have changed beyond all recognition. They are fulfilled in their entirety by heaven, eternity and God.

---

[57] See footnote 2. The literal meaning of the word is 'what may not be set foot upon', from the Greek a- (privative) and the verb *vaino* (βαίνω), to walk or go.

While in terms of society and the world Mount Athos admits only what is absolutely necessary, as far as its spiritual longings are concerned it works on the basis of unlimited excess. All its safeguards and limits are to do with anything secular. The restrictions and laws are there not to forbid someone from doing something, but to protect the right of others to 'delight in the statutes of the Lord and not forget His word, to keep His testimonies, to learn His righteous ordinances'.[58] They are there principally to keep—even if in only one place in the world—the yeast of truth alive, the seed of discernment intact and inner experience genuine. Athos is not held up on the axis of the rights of the individual, but it operates according to the logic of the rights of God.

Yes! Whatever there is on Athos must be shown to be necessary to its survival, and as desirable for its spiritual life. That is why it has its *avaton* rules; that is why certain things are prohibited. Television is not necessary nor is it, of course, desirable. The same goes for hunting, camping, cinemas, parks, playing fields, sea sports, bars and tavernas. It is also *avaton* to sightseers and tourists, the curious, to any impious presence, however innocent.

As a place Athos is *avaton* to all those to whom

---

[58] Ps. 119: 16, 2, 7.

it is *avaton* in spirit. In this sense, it is a 'no-go' area to men also. It admits only those who come in order to further its own aims, and not their own—they are needed; or those whose purpose of their visit is compatible with its ascetic way of life—they are welcomed. These are the people who may become monks and who sustain Athos. These are the people who allow it to function more easily and who affirm its purpose.

The Holy Mountain is neither a museum nor a place of entertainment. It is not even a place of mission. We go there neither to see nor to be seen, nor even to receive spiritual benefit. It is a place of spiritual violence[59] and asceticism. We go to hide ourselves and to be humbled. The presence of women is not compatible with its needs, its spiritual aspirations, or its purpose or way of life. This does not deprive women of some right. Nor does it protect the rights of the monks and the monasteries for reasons of narrow self-interest. It preserves the right of God: His right to rest somewhere peacefully. The *avaton* of Athos ensures the presence of God somewhere on earth.

This holy and blessed concept is, however, gradually being respected less and less. The Holy Mountain is becoming more and more accessible. It

---

[59] See footnote 44.

is covered in roads full of cars and traffic, and there are grandiose construction projects and noisy machines. One thing brings another. And what do we find? The more roads we build, the greater the threat of desecration to the blessed '*avaton*' of Athos. There are the paths so inspiring of compunction: the more overgrown they become, the more the Mountain becomes impassable by God and untrodden by man. In their picturesque turns and in their peace and lowliness there lies hidden the grace of God. It is revealed as an original thought, a new experience, a newly-found strength to make decisions, a clearly formed aim; or it may manifest itself as a chance meeting with an ascetic, an inexplicable fragrance or an unhoped-for miracle.

The roads brought the cars, and the cars filled the Mountain with visitors who did not share its spirit. The ban on vehicles, which until recently was piously maintained—that is why no road has ever been built to Ouranoupolis—has essentially been lifted. One still might not be able to reach Athos by car from the mainland, but they plough over every corner of Athonite land.

You meet God more easily walking along a path than on the road in a car, with its exhaust fumes, the clouds of dust, and the noise, speed and convenience. 'For the gate is small and the way is narrow that leads to life.'[60] 'Civilization' and the mentality that says needs must be satisfied have destroyed the Mountain's beauty and quietness, and now its *avaton* rule is also under threat.

In treading the paths you feel the drops of dew, you come across butterflies and insects, and you smell transcendental scents—those living reminders of its secret and hidden holiness. You experience the fear of snakes and wild animals, the harshness of nature, and the stillness, but you also tire, sweat or cool down: you give time to yourself and to your aspirations; you have the opportunity to work through all the stimuli assailing you; and your heart is full of joy, emotion and yearning.

Above all, walking on Athos allows you—if you are alone—to face yourself, or—if God grants you that blessing—to meet some unknown hermit. Going by car entails reaching your destination quickly and travelling with others, and naturally it deprives you of the possibility of an unexpected encounter.

The inaccessibility—the *avaton*—of Mount Athos makes it more accessible spiritually. When the feet are replaced by wheels; or exhaust fumes take the place of exertion; or instead of the scents of nature there is the stench of petrol or diesel fumes;

---

[60] Matt.7: 14.

or instead of an animal we see an engine; or instead of feeling the heat of the sun on one's face the dust of the road covers one's hair and clothes; or when we replace what is natural and divine with the arrogance of human achievement: how can this Mountain reveal its accessibility? The mountain that is not trodden by foot cannot be ascended in spirit!

Fortunately in our time Athos is not open to women: but unfortunately it is not closed to the machines that paralyse its spirit and 'wound' its monastic ethos. I say fortunately, for if the roads and the cars may threaten its spirit with paralysis, then the entrance of women would signal its final end. But I also say unfortunately, for while the institutional *avaton* rule in the end is a prohibition on the female sex, the preservation of the spiritual *avaton* abolishes every law, and renders invalid every legal or historical restriction. In other words respect for the eternal and inviolable '*avaton*' rules of Mount Athos makes it fully accessible to every soul that thirsts for the truth, whether male or female. Nowadays women try to assert their right to communicate with the monks of Mount Athos in a worldly way. The monks' mothers and relatives step into the no-go area of Athos through their frequent telephone calls and their need for correspondence. They make their care and concern keenly felt by sending knitted items, homemade cakes, biscuits and pies. On the pretext of piety they go up to the permissible geographical limit on boats, but this transgresses the spiritually acceptable limits of the Mountain.

In the end the soul treads only there where comfort, secularisation, compromise, and the destructive modern notion of 'success' are absent. The heart endures the ascent only when one finds conscious and continual renunciation, faithfulness to those initial monastic vows and the love of what is old, humble and plain. In order for the Holy Mountain to remain accessible to God, His grace and every searching soul, it must draw its limits without negotiation and maintain its *avaton* without compromise.

Chapter 6

COMPARING YESTERDAY WITH TODAY

A little while ago I went to England, where I had been invited to a conference on the Holy Mountain, at which I had to speak on distinctive elements of Athonite spirituality. I plunged into my memory, bringing back to mind my first experiences, and reviving my love and respect for and faith in Athos. I wrote my talk with my whole heart, although I maintained one small reservation: would a contemporary Athonite monk accept what I had written, or would he consider it the product of subjective romanticism and the personal exaggeration of a madcap?

While there I visited the Monastery of St John the Baptist in Essex. How much I liked it there! Here I met Athos in an idealised form. The monastery is in the midst of Western civilization and in the middle of nowhere; it lies unprotected; it does not exercise the 'no-go' rule of the *avaton* forbidding men or women; it lacks self-governance and other privileges; it does not have its own tradition; and it has its own expression of monasticism. But it is rich in theology; its way of life has great simplicity and nobleness; and it is unpretentious and ecumenical in style. The buildings are low—the planning laws do not permit anything higher. It is nothing like the 'towering fortress' that is Simonopetra. Everything is modern and English. One finds an absence of any obvious tradition. Yet everything is so traditional, genuine and sound.

Behind every miracle you look for a saint. Behind the Monastery in Essex you can discern the figure of Fr Sophrony. He is famed for the monastery he founded; renowned for his books; he was a great theologian; he led a saintly life; and he suffered adversity and persecution. He had been an Athonite monk but, accused of being a German spy, he was hounded out of the Mountain and fled to Europe. From the desert of Mount Athos he came to the wasteland of the confusion and delusion of the West. He met his elder, St Silouan, on the Mountain. It was in Europe that he revealed him to the world. Silouan's sanctity had not been recognized by his own age, nor in the holy place of his ascetic struggle according to God. He was welcomed as a saint by the modern world of East and West.

Upon my return to Greece, I had the opportunity once again to visit Mount Athos. Being greatly inspired by the Athonite Monastery of the West that I had just visited I decided to project my recent experience onto the background of one of my most favourite places: the hermitage of an unknown ascetic of the past century. At the entrance to a natural cave, about twenty or thirty metres above the waves, beneath a sheer rock face, which looked as if it had been cut by a knife and slid straight down into the sea, at a point more steep than Karoulia: it was there that this angelic man built (although I do not know how) his ascetic dwelling. Every time I saw it from the sea I felt greatly moved.

Whenever I could I would go and venerate this hermitage from near or afar. It was a place that inspired the greatest contrition, unlike anywhere else in the world. My heart brimmed over and I wondered how it did not burst. I was inspired by its position, the wildness of the landscape and the danger of the approach: one could understand what '*avaton*', or 'untrodden', meant on Mount Athos. Before starting along the path one had to work one's way ten times around one's prayer-rope and to call upon all the angelic orders. The place itself was ascetic: a true *asketerio* of self-discipline and abstinence. It was utterly disconsolate and genuinely inhospitable; a supra-human, magnificent, heroic and divine place; the dwelling of a genuine saint.

You did not need any details of the life of its resident to be persuaded of his holiness. Just to behold his hermitage was enough. Without thinking you asked for his blessing, for you realized that he has boldness before God.

That year, after a gap of a long time, I went back to the hermitage. It had been 'carefully' (or so I had heard) renovated—not restored. It was there that he, this saint unknown to men but known to God, had spent hours standing before, and ecstatic in the presence of, God.

A very good friend of mine, a priest-monk, led me there. A new path had been opened to make the place accessible, and this had been done with care and sensitivity. As I walked along I felt a mixture of awe and anticipation. I wanted to see the men of our age expressing their respect and values through their ability to give life to dead things, to resurrect ruins and to restore a hermitage not on the material level, but as a reminder of a living past that can humble us and wake us up spiritually.

As I reached the end of the path I shuddered: I was gripped by something very deep and powerful; I felt a great sense of disappointment and the strong desire to leave and not to see anything more than what the first glance revealed. But my friend was full of love and enthusiasm for the renovation project, and so I remained silent and unwillingly proceeded to make the traumatic discovery.

Here was a little house—no longer a cave or *asketerio* for practising ascesis—made of skilfully dressed stone covered with a special type of veneer and a paved courtyard with supporting walls and a high wooden fence. The kitchen had eight (if I remember rightly) cupboards along the floor and eight along the wall and there was a luxurious, tiled bathroom. The cell itself had a desk that was so well equipped that it seemed more like an office for a learned university professor who had gone to write his doctorate. Naturally, electricity had been installed and there were sockets and electric lights. The ascetic had collected rainwater in a cistern, which they had retained, although I soon learnt that water was to be brought there in a two-inch pipe so that the future supposed ascetic would not be discomforted. It was now suitable for receiving a bishop: there, in an atmosphere of ascetic and historic romanticism, he would be able to spend a few days' holiday writing, studying and enjoying the idyllic sunsets of Athos. Or a new contemporary 'ascetic' could perhaps take up residence there and have his laptop, his mobile, his cupboards full of special fasting food and whatever else could possibly make his life easier. And there he would live under the rock and of course next to, not inside, the cave.

What a terrible shame! Why could the cell not have been restored without losing its original character? Why did they have to build a courtyard, and get rid of the necessary ascetic narrowness of the landscape? Why did the hermit need a kitchen stocked with enough food for a whole monastery, when it could simply have had a sink and a water pitcher? Why instead of rainwater did you have to drink water that smelt of chlorine and protected you from germs? What was the purpose of this building at the base of a rock and at the entrance to a cave? Who can fathom the reason why the place that spoke of the ascetic spirit has been replaced by the external expression of our suburbanizing age in an inaccessible corner of Athos? Why did we not just do what was easy, and do less, which would have been more—and simply maintain the hermitage of a saint, and instead embark on a project that was expensive, difficult and so improbable, polishing away the greatness of a not-so-distant past?

It was rare for me to feel so wounded in my soul. I was ashamed of our age, an age incapable of producing ascetics and unable even to preserve their traces. It cannot respect their memory and it destroys their way of life and their spirit; it puts to death their true remembrance; it would call decline 'flowering', and destruction 'restoration'. It would impose a decorated caricature upon the lasting yet living image of the past. It quotes the sayings of the Fathers without understanding their wisdom. It would create ascesis without deprivation and promise salvation through crosses that have no relation to the Cross of Golgotha. In constructing monastic dwellings intended to sustain a life centred on heaven and the remembrance of death, it creates buildings that reflect a secular mentality and a vision of earthly life.

Fortunately, however, nature defends itself. The humidity of the cave and the rock falls from above make it a difficult and frightening place to stay. These natural phenomena are, unfortunately, the only reminders of what ascesis means, the only vestiges of that ascetic world that seems to be gradually disappearing and will soon exist only to feed our diseased religious imagination.

We can, however, take consolation from one thing. Quite a few years have passed since the hermitage was reconstructed. It has still not acquired a permanent resident. It remains deserted. Our 'civilisation' and modern technology may have done their work, but they could not obliterate the feelings of dread and awe that its position and the ascetic nature of the landscape inspire. It is a blessing that you can now reach it easily, venerate this holy place and experience the nearness of God's grace, be humbled and examine your conscience. Just as long as you do not think that this was how that holy man lived. The feeling of contrition that the place inspires is enough to speak to the heart and allow you to sense that here the ascetic still goes on living in spirit.

I went down to the harbour to take the boat. At the next monastery an old friend of mine, who was also a monk, boarded. We hadn't seen each other for years. Before even asking how I was, he began telling me that I should pitch into 'papists' at any and every opportunity. They haven't repented, he was saying. But we haven't repented, I thought to myself. That is the whole point of Lent. 'Lord, I have no repentance', we sing. This is why we are urged to imitate the prodigal son, the publican, the thief and the prostitute; in this way we might perhaps learn something. But it seems that we have not understood that either. We monks have been crushed by the steamroller of our age. We look outwards and are judgemental but we are also easily offended. We expect others to show repentance when we do not suspect the absence of our own. We restore by destroying. We think that we are showing respect towards others but in truth we offend them. People are indeed good but they go off on the wrong track. The monks try but they do not practice ascetic struggle. Something is surely very wrong here.

This age cannot be conquered. Its downward course cannot be stopped. You can only step beyond it. A few years ago I spent five and a half months at a cell of Pantokrator Monastery, situated next to Koutloumousiou Monastery. There was an outside privy without any running water. You had to think twice about venturing out there: in winter it was the cold, and in summer the flies. The kitchen had an antiquated sink, next to which stood a wood-fired stove with a trivet. There wasn't even any bottled gas. Even to make a cup of tea or coffee was quite a bother: you needed time and patience to bring the wood and light the fire. Food was kept inside a container with sides made of wire meshing. Instead of a table there was a pile of bricks. Instead of chairs there were wooden crates. Yet everything was so easy. It was certainly not convenient, nor ascetic. But it was a blessed place.

Some gossiped about the fathers there, labelling them as extreme. At the time I wondered how people could live like that: now I glorify God that there are still people who do. They, and others like them, are the only people who remain untouched by our age. They transcend it. Through their way of life and ethos they preserve the true meaning of ascesis, struggle and voluntary deprivation. They make it possible for us to understand the Fathers, to experience the glory of the Holy Mountain, to discern the limits and capabilities of the human person, to feel sorrow at the littleness of our age. They still allow us to hope.

Postscript[61]

Everything that the Holy Mountain has to offer is experienced by monks and pilgrims alike as wonder and surprise, as an unprecedented encounter which cannot but leave one unmoved. Its message transcends human logic. It inspires and stirs within you unexpected visions and hope. How marvellous it is to live the spiritual life as a constant godly surprise!

The whole physical and spiritual environment is unique: the natural world, relics, the calendar and Byzantine time,[62] the way of life and habits, the forms of worship, the *avaton* rule, and the various

---

[61] An extract, here found in slightly altered form, from 'Distinctive Features of Athonite Spirituality', an article published in *Mount Athos: the Sacred Bridge* (Peter Lang AG, Bern, 2005). Originally published in N. Hatzinikolaou, *The Holy Mountain* (in Greek) (Athens, 2000), p. 146.

[62] See footnote 39.

manifestations of the spiritual life. All this is not there in order to give the impression of a strange world, to attract the interest of dissatisfied believers, to offer spiritual fulfilment to frustrated Christians, or to serve as a refuge for souls in need of consolation. It is there to give birth to a wondrous creation, called the 'Athonite' monk.

The Athonite monk 'lives as an overseer of the visible world and an initiator of the invisible and noetic creation; as an image created by God and in the likeness of God; he rejoices in being alive and the delight of his heart is unceasing. His entire self flows in uncreated, spiritual light; his mind is simple, pure, full of love, immortal, free and creative. He is a small god by grace, a king of creation.'[63]

Near him—with his unaffected life, his authentic faith, his spontaneous feelings, his transcendent logic, his otherworldly expressions— you feel different yet related to him, human yet with the potential to become like God, insignificant yet consoled, respectful yet friendly. Near him you forgive, you believe, you are comforted, and you hope. You experience the presence and grace of God, eternity and miracles. Near him you yearn for sanctification. You see him dominated by the

---

[63] Theoklitos of Dionysiou, *Between Heaven and Earth* (in Greek) (Athens, 1986), pp. 21-2.

'newness of knowledge', speaking the dialect of 'other tongues', worthy of receiving 'the secret vision', and benefiting from 'strange hearings'.[64] Near him you live truly. On the Holy Mountain you experience the Holy Spirit. Even today.

---

[64] The third troparion from Pentecost Matins.